The TREE OF LIFE

WITNESS LEE

Living Stream Ministry
Anaheim, California • www.lsm.org

First Edition, June, 1987.

ISBN 0-87083-300-6

Published by

Living Stream Ministry
2431 W. La Palma Ave., Anaheim, CA 92801 U.S.A.
P. O. Box 2121, Anaheim, CA 92814 U.S.A.

Printed in the United States of America

02 03 04 05 06 / 11 10 9 8 7 6 5

CONTENTS

PREFACE

This book is composed of messages given by Brother Witness Lee in Los Angeles, California in the summer of 1965.

Chapter One

THE WAY TO FULFILL GOD'S PURPOSE

Scripture Reading: Gen. 2:7-9; John 1:4; 6:35, 57; 4:14, 24; 6:63

GOD'S PURPOSE

God's economy and God's building both depend on the tree of life. In Genesis 1 there is a full record of God's creation. On the sixth day, God created a man in His own image and then committed man with His own authority (v. 26). Image means the expression. Something in your image is the expression of yourself. God created man in His own image for the purpose of having man as His very expression in this universe and on this earth. God is hidden and invisible, yet God does have a heart's desire to express Himself through man. God did not create a thousand men at one time, but He created just one man. All the descendants of that one man were included in that one man. God created a corporate man in His image to express Himself, so man is the very image, the very expression of God.

Why did God also commit man with His authority? God's purpose is to express Himself, but this purpose of God was greatly frustrated by His enemy. God has an enemy in this universe and on this earth, and this earth has been usurped from the hand of God, robbed away from God. Thus, God had to create a man to deal with His enemy. It is for this purpose that God committed His authority to man, that man may be not only His expression but also His representative, representing Him on this earth as the very authority to deal with His enemy.

God gave authority to Adam for the purpose that he may rule over the earth, and especially that he may rule "over every creeping thing that creepeth upon the earth" (v. 26). The implication here is that God's enemy is embodied in the creeping things. In Genesis 3 the head of the creeping things came in, that is, the serpent, the enemy of God. The serpent in Genesis 3 and the scorpions in Luke 10, representing the sinful and unclean evil spirits, are creeping things. God committed His authority to man that man may have not only the power but also the authority to rule the whole earth and to subdue it. That meant that the earth had been in rebellion and that the rebellious earth had to be subdued. Throughout the sixty-six books of the Bible, there are always these two aspects. God's intention positively is to express Himself through a corporate man, and negatively to deal with His enemy, Satan, through this corporate man. At the end of the Scriptures there is a city called the New Jerusalem (Rev. 21:2). God's image is expressed through that city (21:11; 4:3), and God's authority is exercised through that city (22:5; 21:24-26). That city is the very expression and representation of God.

EATING OF THE TREE OF LIFE

In Genesis 1 there is the purpose, the intention of God, but there is not the way to fulfill God's purpose, the way to attain God's intention. The way is not in Genesis 1 but in Genesis 2, and what is the way? The way is the tree of life (v. 9). After the revelation of the words "image" and "dominion" (authority), there is the word "life" in Genesis 2. How could we created human beings express God if we did not have the life of God? You can take a picture of me, but that picture only has a certain image without life. If God is life within you and lives in you, it is possible for you to live God out, to express God in a full way. The way to fulfill God's purpose is seen in the tree of life. Even the matter of authority to represent God also depends on the tree of life. If you do not have the tree of life, God within you as your life, how can you exercise His authority? For these two aspects of God's purpose, God's expression and God's representation, we need God to be life to us. We need God to live within us that we may be His very expression and His very representation.

Throughout world history, there have been many religions

with many natural concepts. With nearly all the religions there is the same one thought that God is the Creator and that we are the creatures. As the Creator, God is so great, so high, and so far away from us, and we are so little, so low. We have to humble ourselves and even to prostrate ourselves to worship this Creator God. I would not say that this is wrong, but I would ask you to consider what God asked man to do after He had created him. After God created man, He did not say, "Adam, you have to realize you are a little creature, and I am your great Creator. I am always on the throne, and you always have to prostrate yourself to worship Me." There is not such a record in Genesis.

Genesis tells us that after God created man, He put man in front of the tree of life. God did not give man a list of commandments. That was the work of Moses after the fall, not the work of God according to His eternal intention. The law is in Exodus 20, not in Genesis 2. In Genesis 2 is the first picture regarding God's dealing with His created man. There is such a basic principle of the first mentioning in the Bible. Whenever you have the first mentioning, a principle is always laid. The first mentioning of God's dealing with man is that God put Adam in front of the tree of life, charging him to be careful about his eating (vv. 16-17). God's intention for man is not a matter of doing, but a matter of eating. If man eats well and eats rightly, then he will be right.

This tree of life is God in Christ as the Spirit to be life to us. It is the Triune God, the Father in the Son, and the Son as the Spirit. Before we received the Lord, we may not have thought anything about God. But when we got saved or revived, we might have immediately made up our mind to serve the Lord, to do our best to do good deeds to please Him, and to "go to church" to worship Him. These thoughts, which are according to our natural concept, are wrong. God's intention is not that we serve Him, do good to please Him, or that we worship Him in a religious, ritualistic way. But God's intention is that we eat Him. We have to eat Him. The first picture of God's dealing with man is not a picture of doing, but a picture of eating.

God presented Himself to man in the form of food. This can be clearly seen in the Gospel of John. John tells us that in the beginning was the Word, the Word was God, and in Him was life (1:1, 4). One day He performed a miracle by feeding five thousand people with five barley loaves and two fishes (6:9-13). Then the people wanted to make Him a king. But He did not take that offer (v. 15). He later told them that He came not to be a king to rule others outwardly but to be the bread of life to be eaten (vv. 35, 57). He came that we may eat Him. The Lord does not want us to consider how to serve Him, how to worship Him, or how to glorify Him, but He wants us to consider Him as our food. He came to present Himself to us as life in the form of food. We have to take Him as food by feeding on Him and eating Him. "He who eats Me shall also live because of Me" (v. 57b).

We have to believe in the Lord Jesus because we need Him as our life (3:16, 36). To believe in Him is to receive Him into us as life (1:12-13). He is not only our objective Savior but also our subjective life. We need such a life. After receiving Him, the problem with us is not related to work, to service, or to worship, but to eating. How do you eat, what do you eat, and how much do you eat? Immediately after the creation of man, God put man in front of the tree of life that man may take the tree of life as his food. This simply means that God presented Himself to man as life in the form of food. God had no intention to ask man to do things for Him. God's intention is that man would simply take God Himself as his food, that man would feed on God.

CHANGING OUR CONCEPT FROM DOING TO EATING

I hope that the Lord would change your concept from doing to eating. If you would become not merely a doing Christian but an eating Christian, that would be wonderful. In today's Christianity the emphasis is on doing and working. Christianity has been degraded into a doing religion, a working religion, a toiling religion. But God's first intention is not to have man toiling, but to have man feasting and feeding on Him, to have man enjoying God Himself. John 4:24 tells us that we must worship God, but we must ask what the word "worship" means. According to the full context of John 4, the Lord's meaning is that to drink of Him as the living water in

verse 14 is to worship Him in verse 24. When you drink of
Him as the living water, that means that you worship Him.
The more you drink of Him, the more you will be filled with
Him and the more He will be worshipped by you. The best
way to worship the Lord is to drink of Him, to feed on Him, to
enjoy Him, to take Him in.

To say that we should not be doing Christians anymore
but eating Christians may be easy. You may say this, but your
prayers to the Lord may remain the same. You may still pray,
"Lord, help me today to do the right thing. Lord, You know my
weakness, You know how easily I lose my temper. Lord, help
me today not to lose my temper." This prayer shows that you
are still in the concept of doing. If you would be willing to be
delivered from this matter of doing, that would be a "real miracle." You have to see the vision. Once the Lord enlightens
you, you will say, "Lord I want nothing to do with doing, so I
won't ask You to help me do anything. But help me to feed on
You, to eat You." I have been learning this lesson for more
than fifty years. At times I drifted back. Whenever I began to
ask the Lord to help me, I immediately had to stop myself and
have a turn to tell the Lord, "O Lord, I open myself to You.
You are my enjoyment."

We may realize that we need to forget about doing, but it
is not so easy for us to forget. This matter of doing is in our
blood. It is very hard for us to get rid of this. We must see that
right after the Lord's creation of man, He put man before
Himself and presented Himself as the tree of life in the form
of food. We all have to learn how to feed on the Lord, how to
eat of Him. In China it is very hard for people who believe in
the teachings of Confucius to forget about doing. We all have
to first realize that the Lord has no intention that we do
something for Him. The Lord's intention is to present Himself
as food to us day by day. In the Gospel of John, the Lord is
first seen as life (1:4), as the bread of life (6:35), as the water
of life (4:14), and as the breath of life, the air (20:22). He is
life, food, drink, and air. All this is not for you to be a doing
Christian but to be an enjoying Christian. You have to enjoy
the Lord as life, as food, as water, and as air. You have to

breathe Him in, to drink of Him, and to feed on Him in order
to live by Him and in Him.

HOW TO ENJOY CHRIST

We also have to learn how to enjoy Him. He is life, food,
water, and air to us, but how can we enjoy Him? If we are
going to enjoy the Lord, we have to open ourselves, not superficially but in a deep way. We should not only open our mind,
or even our heart, but we also have to open our spirit. You may
say that you are so open to the Lord. But how open are you,
and how deeply do you open to the Lord? A brother may seem
to be open to everybody, but he may only be open superficially.
He is not open deeply. Many times when we come to the Lord,
we just open our mind but not our whole heart. Sometimes we
may open our heart, but some deep part within us may still be
closed. We have to open ourselves from the depths of our
being. If we would learn to enjoy the Lord, we have to learn
this one lesson—how to open ourselves. We have to open ourselves by opening our mind, our heart, and eventually by
opening our spirit. We have to open the depths of our entire
being to the Lord.

I once thought that to drink of the Lord meant that the
Lord was outside of me. But later on from experience and from
the reading of the Word, especially John 4, I found that to
drink of the Lord is not in this way. Since the time we received
the Lord, the Lord as the very spring of living water is within
us. Do not consider that the spring is in the heavens or that it
is something outside of you. You have to realize that the Lord
as the living water is within you as the living spring in the
deepest part of your being. He is in your spirit. John 4:14 says,
"The water that I shall give him shall become in him a spring
of water welling up into eternal life." In this verse we should
underline the words "in him." This spring is "in him," in us. In
what part of us? John 4:24 says, "God is Spirit; and those who
worship Him must worship in spirit...." If you read the whole
context of John 4, you will realize that this living water, the
spring within us, is in our spirit. If you are going to drink
of the Lord, do not think that the Lord as someone outside of
you will come into you. The Lord is within you already in your

spirit. Now you have to learn to open yourself. Open your mind, your heart, and your spirit to the Lord. Then the spring will well up. When this spring wells up and springs up, it will water you and you will drink of Him. This spring is not something from outside, but is something from within the depths of your being, your spirit. You have this living spring within you, but this living spring may be shut up, concealed, confined, and closed deep within you. There is no need for Him to come in, but there is a need for you to open yourself that He may well up. When He springs up within you, you will be watered. The problem today is that we Christians do not have this vision. We merely thought that the Lord is the Creator, the very God, whom we have to fear, love, and serve; we have to do something to please Him, and we have to worship Him. We did not realize that He is everything to us. He is our life, our life supply, our food, our drink, and our air for our enjoyment. Today the tree of life is not outside of us but within us. We have such a living supply within us, so now we have to learn how to open ourselves to the Lord as our living, inward life supply.

We should pray, "Lord, help me to open myself to You." To open yourself is not so easy. If you try to do this, you will find out where you are. You may only open to a certain degree. You may not open deeply. You have to learn the lesson to try to open yourself. For a person to be saved by the Lord in a strong way depends upon how much he would repent. This means it depends upon how deeply this person would open himself to the Lord. We may have been saved for many years, and we may have learned many lessons with the Lord, but even today we still need to learn one lesson—to open ourselves from the depths of our being. If you would go to the Lord and pray, "Lord, help me to open myself to You," then you will see that the living water will spring up within you and flow out. This flow of the living water brings you the supply of life. Do not try to do the right thing, but you have to try to open yourself to the Lord from deep within.

We must learn to come to the Lord in a new way. We must learn how to contact the Lord by opening ourselves from within. You have to say, "Lord, help me to open my mind, to open my heart, and even to open my spirit, to open my entire being, the depths of my being, to You. Lord, reveal Your riches to me and impart Yourself into me that I may enjoy You." If you would open yourself to the Lord in such a way, you will see how real, available, and precious the Lord is. You will sense His presence within, and you will be filled with Him. He is not only the life to you, but He is also the food (the bread of life), the drink (the water of life), and the air (the breath of life) to you. All these things are related to the Lord as the tree of life. You have to learn how to take Him in, how to enjoy Him, how to feed on Him, how to drink of Him, and even how to breathe Him in. There is only one way for you to do this—learn to open yourself.

Open yourself to the Lord and learn to stay with Him for some time. During this time, forget about your needs, your business, your family, your home affairs, your work, and everything else. Just open yourself to the Lord and enjoy Him for a length of time. Feed on Him, drink of Him, and breathe Him in. Regardless of how busy we are, we have to spend three times a day to sit down to eat something. The most healthy practice is to pay full attention to what you are eating and not to anything else. If you try to take care of other things while you are eating, your enjoyment of the food will be limited and you may not digest it so well. Sometimes I do not like to receive phone calls while I am eating. Likewise, while I am praying and having a time with the Lord, I do not like to receive phone calls. We all need to set apart a time, free from all outside disturbances, in which we open our entire being to the Lord just to enjoy Him.

Learn to contact the Lord by realizing that He is your food, your drink, and your air. You have to enjoy Him. You have to feed on Him, drink of Him, and breathe Him in. Then your Christian life will be healthy, and you will be normal. We are somewhat abnormal because we are too active in doing, too active in working, but very passive in eating and enjoying the Lord. We do not enjoy the Lord so much, so we have a very poor expression of the Lord and a very weak representation of the Lord. If we would feed on the Lord properly and adequately, drink of the Lord richly and deeply, and breathe the

Lord all the time from the depths of our being, we will be so strong in the expression of the Lord and in the representation of the Lord.

We need to retire and resign from doing, from working, from toiling, from laboring. We have to be retired to Him and resigned to Him. Learn to go to Him to spend some time. Retire from your job for the Lord, from all your activities for the Lord. I found the secret that if you are going to retire yourself from all things to the Lord, you have to learn how to open yourself, the deeper the better. You have to open yourself from the depths of your being. Learn to do this one thing. Then the Lord's image and authority will be with you by the way of life. The living water will have a way to spring up within you by your opening yourself. You are the barrier, you are the hindrance, and you are the dirt. You have to dig away so that the spring of living water can well up within you.

Learn to open yourself. Then you will enjoy the Lord as the tree of life. With the tree of life is the flow of living water and the fresh air as the breath of life. If you open yourself to the Lord, the Lord will spring up from within you. Then you will be nourished, watered, refreshed, and strengthened from within. You will be right in your person, in your being, in what you are, not just in what you do. May the Lord bring us into His intention, that is, into the enjoyment of Himself as our life and life supply that we may express Him in His image and represent Him with His authority on the earth.

CHAPTER TWO

THE SOURCE AND CONSUMMATION
OF THE TWO TREES

Scripture Reading: Gen. 2:7-9; 3:2-7; 4:16-22; 6:3, 5; 7:17-24; 11:1-9; 1 Cor. 6:17; Matt. 16:22-25; Rev. 20:10, 14-15; 21:2; 22:1-2

It would be a great help to us to see a brief picture of the tree of life throughout the entire Bible. The Bible starts with two trees and also ends with the result of the two trees. It starts in the same way that it ends.

THE THREE PARTIES IN THE UNIVERSE

In the universe there are three parties: God, Satan, and man. Man is in between God and Satan. After man was created by God, he was neutral to God and to Satan. In Genesis, God is represented by the tree of life. God presented Himself to man as the tree of life, so the tree of life is the reality of God. There is another tree, the tree of knowledge, representing Satan. Man, created by God with a spirit, soul, and body (2:7), was neutral between these two trees. The three parties in Genesis 2 are God, represented by the tree of life, Satan, the very source of death, represented by the tree of knowledge, and man, who was created by God in three parts. Genesis 2:7 says that "the Lord God formed man of the dust of the ground, and breathed into his nostrils the breath of life; and man became a living soul." This verse shows the tripartite man with the body formed of the dust of the ground, the spirit as the breath of life, and the soul, which was formed when both the spirit and the body came together. Between God and Satan there was and still is a struggle. God is going to perform and fulfill His purpose, and Satan is doing his best to frustrate God's purpose. All the incidents recorded in the sixty-six books of the Scriptures came either out of the tree of life through man or out of the tree of knowledge through man.

THE TWO MINGLINGS

Before man contacted the tree of life by exercising his spirit, Satan came in and man was tempted to partake of the tree of knowledge. God's intention was that the tree of life would get into the spirit of man, but before this the tree of knowledge got into the soul of man. Thus, there was a mingling of Satan with man's soul. All the evil things and sinful stories came out of this mingling of Satan with man in man's soul. This mingling is the very source of all the evil, sinful things on this earth. Genesis 3 gives a record of this mingling, and in Genesis 4 are seen the consequences of this mingling. The result of the mingling of Satan with man's soul was a city built up with a culture (vv. 16-22). Cain named the city after his son Enoch. In that culture man became flesh and all mankind was corrupted with evil (6:3, 5). Due to the corruption of that sinful culture, God sent the flood to judge the human race (7:17-24). A further result of this satanic force with man's soulish power is that of Babel (11:1-9). Babel was the issue of the mingling of Satan with man's soulish power. The negative stories of Sodom and Egypt, and all the sinful events recorded in Genesis and Exodus came out of this mingling of Satan with man's soul.

In the Bible there is a line of the satanic work and another line of God's work. The enemy of God is working all the time by injecting himself into man's soul. All the evil things and sinful stories come out of the mingling of Satan with man's soul, the working of Satan into man, with man, and through man. At the same time God works. God's work is to work Himself into man's spirit. All the holy things and spiritual stories come out of another mingling, the mingling of God with man's spirit. Eventually in the New Testament there is this verse, 1 Corinthians 6:17, which says, "He who is joined to the Lord is one spirit." Since the Lord Himself is the Spirit (2 Cor. 3:17) and has created us with a spirit (Rom. 8:16), we can be joined to Him as one spirit. The story of Abel testifies of a man who did not live in the soul but in the spirit. The accounts of Enosh, Enoch, Noah, Abraham, Isaac, Jacob, and Joseph also testify of people who were not living by their reasoning in their soul but who were living by the faith in the spirit.

The children of Israel, the descendants of the Patriarchs, wandered away from God's way, but since the day God delivered them from Egypt on the day of the Passover, they were taught not to live in a worldly or natural way. They had to live on the lamb. They had to slay the lamb, apply the blood of the lamb, and eat the meat of the lamb. They also learned how to live by eating the unleavened bread. After they came out of Egypt, they were wandering in the wilderness and were taught to live on the heavenly manna. Their living was absolutely different from the worldly and natural way to live. This means that they learned not to live in themselves but to live in the Lord. The lamb of the Passover, the unleavened bread, and the heavenly manna on which the children of Israel lived are types of Christ. Furthermore, all the offerings related to the tabernacle and all the things included in the tabernacle are types of Christ. This provides us with a full picture showing the way to live in the spirit, to live not by ourselves but by the Lord.

The children of Israel could not be saved by themselves and they even could not live by themselves. They had to be saved by the blood of the Passover lamb, and they had to live by the Passover lamb. In the wilderness they had to live day by day on the heavenly manna. Whatever they lived on was a real type of Christ. The pillar of fire and the pillar of cloud are types of Christ. The rock from which the living water came out to quench their thirst was also a type of Christ. Moses and Joshua, the leaders of the children of Israel, were types of Christ. All these types signify that we should not live according to anything of ourselves; we have to live by Christ. All the worldly people have been occupied and gained by Satan. According to the picture in the Old Testament, only a minority, the children of Israel, were occupied and gained by God. They learned to live, to exist, to move, to have their being, not according to the worldly way but according to the heavenly way. That means they did not live by themselves but they lived by the Lord.

Thus, we see a picture of two minglings: first, the mingling of Satan in the soul of man, and second, the mingling of God in the spirit of man. All events throughout the history of the human race have come out of either one or the other. God's intention is to work Himself into us so that He will be everything to us. But Satan's intention is to work himself into man to make a counterfeit of the mingling of God with man. Satan does not focus his attention on what we do or on what we try to accomplish. Satan's intention is to frustrate us from touching God and from being mingled with God. If he can frustrate this, he would allow us to do good and religious things and would even utilize the religious things to frustrate us from being mingled with God.

This is confirmed by the history of the children of Israel. In the early years of their history they learned how to live not by themselves but by the Lord as everything. Everything related to them in the Pentateuch was a type of Christ, showing that the Lord became everything to them, that they lived not by themselves but by the Lord. Eventually, they departed from the Lord Himself and used the things in the Pentateuch as rules and regulations, forming a religion out of the types and shadows of Christ. They were deceived by good and religious things and captured from the Lord to something other than Himself. This is what we call the Jewish religion. This Jewish religion can be seen in both the Old and New Testaments. According to the record of the four Gospels, we can realize how much the enemy, Satan, utilized the Jewish religion to frustrate people from contacting and enjoying the Lord Himself. Satan, the enemy of God, took the very things that God used to bring people to Himself to form a Jewish religion, which he used as a substitute to replace Christ, who is the embodiment of God, in their experience.

When the Lord Jesus came, He was the reality of all the types in the Pentateuch. There are so many items in the Pentateuch, but in the four Gospels there is one person who is all-inclusive. He is the Lamb of God, the unleavened bread, the heavenly manna, the tabernacle with all the offerings, and everything. He is the all-inclusive One. When He presented Himself to the Jews, most would not receive Him because the Jewish people were distracted from Him by their religion and even by the Old Testament. The scribes and Pharisees used the Scriptures to argue frequently with the Lord Jesus. The Holy Scriptures were given by God to bring people to Himself, but even these Scriptures were utilized by God's enemy to frustrate people from contacting the Lord Himself. The Jewish religionists searched the Scriptures for knowledge, yet they would not come to the Lord Jesus for life (John 5:39-40). This meant that they attached themselves to the tree of knowledge, spending much time in searching, studying, and learning the Scriptures, yet they would not come to the Lord Jesus as the tree of life for life. They attached themselves to something other than the Lord Himself.

The same problem continued in the book of Acts. The church began with a group of people receiving Christ and taking Christ as their life. The church was started and formed in this way. However, the book of Acts with the following Epistles show us that even in the church among the Christians, Satan could utilize so-called Christian things to frustrate and distract people from the Lord Himself. The matter of divisions among the Lord's children was used by the enemy to frustrate their oneness in Christ.

The divisions came out of two categories of things—teachings and gifts. The Epistles show us that it was due to the teachings and the gifts that divisions began to exist among the Christians. The teachings and the gifts are both good. If they were not good, Christians would not accept them. Paul points out in 1 Timothy that the different teachings are the seed, the source, of the church's decline, degradation, and deterioration (1:3-4, 6-7; 6:3-5, 20-21). In the church at Corinth there were divisions mostly due to the gifts. The teachings and gifts are good, but we have to realize that they both must be for Christ. Teachings should not be for teachings, and gifts should not be for gifts. All the teachings and gifts must be for Christ. The teachings and gifts must only be a means to convey Christ and should not be an end in themselves. Satan, the subtle one, came

in to utilize even the good teachings and the proper gifts to
seduce people from Christ.

Finally, at the end of the Scriptures, in Revelation, the
worldly system is portrayed as being married to religion. The
worldly civilization is pictured as a husband, and religion is likened to a harlot. This is why there is a picture in the book of
Revelation of a woman, a harlot, sitting on a beast (17:3). The
beast represents the ultimate consummation of all human
inventions resulting in institutions and politics and upon that
beast is a woman representing religion. The great mysterious
Babylon is a mixture of human civilization with religion. If we
are not clear about this vision, it will be easy for us to be
seduced from the way of life into something other than the Lord
Himself.

Satan injected himself into the soul of man and became
mingled with man's soul. Out of this mingling come all the
sinful, evil stories throughout the history of the human race.
We have to realize that to live in our soul and deal with religion is a serious matter. Even religion can be utilized by
Satan. If we have a clear vision from the Lord, we will see that
today many Christians along with Christian activities, religious movements, and Christian doings are utilized by the
enemy of God to frustrate people from the tree of life, which is
a figure of Christ.

EXPERIENCING CHRIST
AS THE TREE OF LIFE IN OUR SPIRIT

On the positive side, there is another line in the New Testament, the line of the mingling of God with the spirit of man. We
are charged to walk in the spirit, to live in the spirit, to do
things in the spirit, to pray in the spirit. This is not a mere
phrase. When we live in our spirit, we will not live by ourselves
but by the Lord. When we learn to walk according to our spirit,
we will not walk according to the worldly system but according to the heavenly way. According to the record of the New
Testament, even the teachings and gifts by themselves are cate-
gorized with the tree of knowledge. With the tree of knowledge
are knowledge, good, evil, and death. This tree is complicated.
But with the tree of life there is only one item and nothing

else—life, life, life. The tree of life is so simple. The Scriptures reveal life as the beginning, life as the process, life as the ending, and life as everything. It is possible that our good doings may not be related to life but fully related and wrapped up with the tree of the knowledge of good and evil. The Lord is not merely interested in what we are doing, but in whether we are in our soul or in our spirit. This is why the Lord told us emphatically in the four Gospels many times that we have to deny the soul, the self. This is because Satan is mingled with our soul, with our self. In Matthew 16, Peter thought that he was saying something good to the Lord, but the Lord rebuked him, calling him Satan (vv. 22-23). Christ perceived that it was not Peter but Satan who frustrated Him from taking the cross. Immediately after this the Lord talked about denying the self and losing the soul-life (vv. 24-25). This proves that Satan is one with our soul, one with our self.

Only the experiences of the Lord Himself in our spirit will last eternally. The teachings will not remain; they will pass away. Our primary need is not for more knowledge about the Lord. What we need today is to contact the Lord. Our need today is not for gifts, but for the Lord Himself as our life, our food, our drink, and our air. We have to realize the Lord Himself in such a full and all-inclusive way. Then we will have the proper and living knowledge of the Lord, not from letters but from life. If we would experience the Lord in such a way, we will then have the proper function. The proper function and the proper gifts will come out of the inner life.

It is good that we retire from things other than the Lord Himself. We must learn to return ourselves to the Lord Himself. With the tree of the knowledge of good and evil everything is complicated. Good and evil are mixed together and result in death. The one thing we need is to enjoy the Lord as the tree of life. We have to learn how to enjoy, to partake of, this living Lord. We have to learn how to contact Him, how to realize Him, and how to experience Him in the spirit as our life and everything.

THE ULTIMATE CONSUMMATION OF THE TWO TREES

All the positive things come out of the experience of the tree of life, out of the mingling of Christ as life with our spirit. The church, the kingdom, the New Jerusalem, and all the positive spiritual heavenly things come out of the mingling of God with our spirit, that is, out of the experience of the tree of life. The ultimate consummation of the tree of knowledge is the lake of fire (Rev. 20:10, 14-15), and the ultimate consummation of the tree of life is the city of water, the New Jerusalem (21:2). This city is characterized by a pure river of water of life, with the tree of life in its flow (22:1-2). All the things of man related to the tree of knowledge, related to Satan, will go into the lake of fire, and the things of man related to God, to the tree of life, will go into the city of living water. We need to spend our time to read the New Testament once more with this point of view, the point of view in the spirit.

CHAPTER THREE

THE TREE OF LIFE
IN THE GOSPEL OF JOHN

Scripture Reading: John 1:4; 14:6; 8:12; 6:35; 7:37-39; 4:14; 20:22; 15:5

We have seen that after God created man, He put him in front of the tree of life. God's intention was that man would partake of the tree of life, which signifies God in Christ through the Holy Spirit as life to us in the form of food. Man did not contact the tree of life, however, because the enemy of God, Satan, came in to seduce man from the tree of life and deceive him to take another source, the tree of knowledge. With this tree of knowledge there is not only evil but also good. It is the tree of the knowledge of good and evil resulting in death. Man was seduced, tempted, to partake of this tree of knowledge, and man fell.

THE ENJOYMENT OF CHRIST IN THE OLD TESTAMENT

After the fall of man, the first thing God did for man was to provide a sacrifice. Adam enjoyed and partook of that sacrifice (Gen. 3:21). Following Adam, Abel partook of the same sacrifice (4:4). Noah built an altar and offered sacrifices (8:20). Later, Abraham followed the same steps: he built an altar and offered a sacrifice (12:7-8). Isaac (26:24-25) and Jacob (35:1, 7) also followed in the steps of their forefathers to build an altar and offer a sacrifice. The first major aspect of Christ the children of Israel enjoyed was the Passover lamb (Exo. 12:3-7). From Adam to the children of Israel, the people who were chosen, elected, by God enjoyed the same sacrifice.

From Exodus 12 the children of Israel began to enjoy the lamb, which is a type of Christ. Christ Himself is the unique sacrifice, the Lamb of God, who takes away the sin of the world (John 1:29). The lamb in Exodus 12 has two aspects—the blood for redeeming outwardly and the meat for nourishing inwardly. The blood is the redeeming aspect of the lamb, and the meat is the nourishing aspect of the lamb. It was through Christ as the Lamb of God that we were brought back to enjoy Him as the tree of life once again. With the sacrifice of the Passover lamb, the children of Israel enjoyed the unleavened bread and the bitter herbs (v. 8). Then they enjoyed the pillar of cloud by day, the pillar of fire by night (13:21-22), the heavenly manna (16:31), and the living water from the cleft rock (17:6). Eventually they enjoyed all the offerings (Lev. 6:8—7:34), the priesthood (Exo. 40:13-15), the tabernacle (25:9), all the riches of the good land (Deut. 8:7-10), and finally in the fullest way they enjoyed Christ as the temple (1 Kings 7:51). The Passover lamb, the unleavened bread, the bitter herbs, the heavenly manna, the living water, the different types of offerings, and the rich produce of the good land are all different aspects of the tree of life. Remember that the entire Old Testament tells us one thing—that God first presented Himself as the tree of life to us that we may partake of Him as food and that we may enjoy Him as our life and everything. After man fell, God provided the lamb for man to be redeemed, and eventually God became the very temple to man.

CHRIST AS THE LAMB OF GOD AND THE TEMPLE

One day the Triune God, who is the reality of the tree of life and of all the other positive items in the Old Testament, came to be a man. He was incarnated. The Gospel of John tells us that in the beginning was the Word, the Word was God, and the Word became flesh (1:1, 14). John 1:29 tells us that this One is the Lamb of God. In John 2 the Lord reveals that He is the temple (vv. 20-22).

In Psalm 23 we first enjoy the Lord as the living pasture (v. 2), and finally we enjoy the Lord as the temple. The psalmist says, "I will dwell in the house of the Lord for ever" (v. 6). The temple is not only the dwelling place of God but also a dwelling place to us, God's seeking ones. In John 15 the Lord Jesus told us that we have to abide in Him; then He will abide in us (vv. 4-5). We become an abode to Him, and He becomes an abode to us. This is a mutual abode. He is our abode, our dwelling place, our temple (Rev. 21:22). In John 14 He told us that in His Father's house are many abodes (v. 2). The Lord is our abode, and we are His abodes. This mutual abode indicates the mingling of the Lord as the Spirit (2 Cor. 3:17) with us in our spirit. "He who is joined to the Lord is one spirit" (1 Cor. 6:17). The divine Spirit and the human spirit are mingled together as one spirit, and this mingling is the mutual abode. We are the Lord's abode, and He is our abode; He and we are mingled together.

THE SON BEING THE FATHER

We need to read the Gospel of John again to find out all the items that the Lord Jesus is to us. John tells us that the Word, who was God, became a man of flesh. Who is this Christ? This Christ is the very God incarnated as a man. He is the complete God and the perfect man, the God-man. Isaiah 9:6 says, "For unto us a child is born, unto us a son is given: and the government shall be upon his shoulder: and his name shall be called Wonderful, Counselor, The mighty God, The everlasting Father, The Prince of Peace." Christ as the very God incarnated to be a man was a child born to us and a son given to us. The Gospel of John tells us clearly that Christ is the very Son of God, but Isaiah 9:6 does not only tell us that a child is born to us whose name is called the mighty God. Isaiah 9:6 also tells us that a son is given to us whose name is called the everlasting Father.

In John 14 Philip asked the Lord Jesus to show the disciples the Father, and then they would be satisfied. Jesus responded to Philip, "Am I so long a time with you, and you have not known Me, Philip? He who has seen Me has seen the Father. How is it that you say, Show us the Father? Do you not believe that I am in the Father, and the Father is in Me?" (vv. 9-10). The Father is in the Son, and the Son is the very expression of the Father. The Son cannot be separated from the Father.

Because of the limitation of our human language in describing the mystery of the divine Trinity, we may say that the Son and the Father are two persons of the Godhead, but we cannot say that they are two separate persons. These are two persons

in one reality. You can never separate the Son from the Father.
If you do not have the Son, you do not have the Father (1 John
2:23). If you have the Son, you have the Father because the
Father is in the Son and the Son is the very expression, the very
embodiment, and the very reality of the Father. In John 10:30
the Lord Jesus said, "I and the Father are one."

THE LORD BEING THE SPIRIT

John 14 reveals that the Son is the Father and then goes
on to reveal that the Son is the Spirit. The Lord tells the disciples that He will ask the Father to give them another
Comforter and that this Comforter is "the Spirit of reality,
whom the world cannot receive, because it does not behold
Him or know Him; but you know Him, because He abides
with you and shall be in you" (v. 17). The Lord continues in
verse 18, "I will not leave you orphans; I am coming to you."
The very "He" who is the Spirit of reality in verse 17, becomes
the very "I" who is the Lord Himself in verse 18. This means
that after His resurrection the Lord became the Spirit of reality. First Corinthians 15:45 confirms this. In dealing with the
matter of resurrection, it says, "The last Adam became a
life-giving Spirit." Isaiah 9:6 is a strong verse to prove that
the Son is the Father. A son is given to us, yet His name is
called the everlasting Father. Another strong verse to prove
that the Son is the Spirit is 2 Corinthians 3:17 which says,
"The Lord is the Spirit." Second Corinthians 3:6 says, "The
letter kills, but the Spirit gives life." Thus, the Lord is the
Spirit that gives life, the life-giving Spirit.

In John 20 the Lord Jesus came to His disciples after His
resurrection, breathed into them, and said to them, "Receive
the Holy Spirit" (v. 22). The breath out of the Lord is the very
Holy Spirit. Christ was incarnated to be the embodiment of
the Triune God, and He became the Spirit who is the transmission of the Triune God. By the Spirit, the Lord transmits
all that He is into our being. The word for spirit in Greek,
pneuma, can also mean wind, breath, or air. The Spirit today
is like the air that we breathe. Without air, our life would be
over in a matter of minutes. The air is marvelous. Its expanse
is so great, yet it is so available. The Lord Jesus to us is just

like the air. He breathed into the disciples and told them to receive the Holy Spirit. Our Christ is not only the Savior, the Redeemer, the Lamb who was slain, crucified, on the cross, but He is also the very God in the Son, with the Father as His reality and the Spirit as His transmission. He comes into us as the Spirit like the air, so vast and yet so available and real. This Spirit as the air is the full reality of the Triune God.

SIX MAJOR ITEMS OF CHRIST FOR OUR ENJOYMENT

For us to live, we need life, light, food, drink, air, and an abiding place to rest. The Lord is all of these items to us. Although there are many other items of Christ in John's Gospel, these are the six major items for our enjoyment. Christ is our life (1:4; 14:6), but for life to be maintained there is the need of Christ as our light (1:4; 8:12), food (6:35), drink (7:37-39; 4:14), air (20:22), and an abiding place (15:5). All these items are different aspects of Christ as the tree of life. We need to be impressed that the Lord is the embodiment of the Triune God realized as the Spirit to be everything to us. I hope this fellowship will enlarge our apprehension and our vision of the Lord Jesus. I came to know Him in a living way many years ago, but when I was a young believer, I did not know the Lord in such a full way. We need to tell the Lord, "O Lord, You are everything to me." We need the heavenly vision to see all the different aspects of Christ in the Word.

According to our experience, when we breathe the Lord in as the fresh air, we also enjoy Him as the water. In this water we have Him as food, and in this food we have Him as light. Learn to breathe Him in. The more you breathe Him in, the more you will have Him as the dew to water you. In the living water is the tree of life growing, the food, and with this food there is always the light. The water is in the air, the food is in the water, and the light is with the food. The more you breathe Him in, the more you will be watered. The more you are watered, the more you will be nourished. And the more you are nourished, the more you will be enlightened. You will be in the light and be full of light. We need to enjoy the Lord in such a way. When we go to the Lord to spend personal time with Him, we have many aspects of His wonderful person for which to praise Him.

BORN OF GOD IN OUR SPIRIT

John 1:12 says that "as many as received Him, to them He gave authority to become children of God." Because we have received Christ, we have been born "not of blood, nor of the will of the flesh, nor of the will of man, but of God" (v. 13). As many as received Christ were born of God. When we initially received Christ as the tree of life, a birth occurred and a life relationship with God was established. When I received Christ as my Savior, I only realized that I was a sinner who was saved from eternal perdition. I did not realize that Christ was life to me and that I had a life relationship established with the Father God. We need to realize that when we received Christ, we were born of God, and God was born into us. As those who have been born of God, we have a life relationship with God.

Now we have to go on to find out what part of our being this birth was accomplished in. Were we born of God in our mind, our body, or our heart? Some say that the heart and the spirit are the same. But the Bible reveals that the heart and the spirit are distinct entities. Ezekiel 36:26-27 says, "A new heart also will I give you, and a new spirit will I put within you: and I will take away the stony heart out of your flesh, and I will give you a heart of flesh. And I will put my Spirit within you...." The new heart in these verses is different from the new spirit, and this new spirit is not God's Spirit because in verse 27 the Lord says, "my Spirit." These are three things—a new heart, a new spirit, and my Spirit. You cannot say that the heart is the spirit. We need a new heart, and we also need a new spirit.

In John 4:24 the Lord Jesus did not say that God is Spirit and those who worship Him must worship Him in the heart. We must worship God in spirit. John 3:6 says, "That which is born of the flesh is flesh, and that which is born of the Spirit is spirit." Our second birth, our spiritual birth, which happened when we received Christ, was accomplished in our spirit. To be born of the Spirit means to be born of God. We were regenerated, reborn, in our spirit. Before we were regenerated, we were dead in our spirit (Eph. 2:1). When we received Christ by calling upon the name of the Lord, Christ as the Spirit came into us just like the air.

This living One, this spiritual air, is so wonderful. All of the processes that the Triune God has passed through, including incarnation, human living, crucifixion, resurrection, and ascension, are included in this air along with all that the Triune God is, has accomplished, attained, and obtained. Whenever a sinner opens himself to the Lord saying, "Lord, I am a sinner. Forgive me of all my sins and come into me to be my life," the living air, the breath of life, the Holy Spirit, the very reality of the Triune God incarnated as a man, comes into this person to make his deadened spirit alive and impart the Triune God into his spirit. Now all that the Triune God is is in this person. May the Lord grant us all a revelation of this wonderful, all-inclusive Triune God indwelling our spirit.

OPENING OURSELVES TO THE LORD

John 3:6 tells us that we were born of God in our spirit. And John 4:14 says, "The water that I shall give him shall become in him a spring of water...." The small phrase "in him" is crucial in John 4:14. This living spring of water is Christ, the very embodiment of the processed Triune God, who has become the life-giving Spirit in our spirit. As the spring of living water, the Lord is always waiting for a chance to well up within us. Since you initially received the Lord, you may not have opened to Him from the depths of your being. If this is true, your spirit has become a prison, a jail, to Christ. Christ may be imprisoned in you. You may be thirsty because the fountain, the spring, is closed within you. There is no flow.

If you expect that the Lord will quench you from the heavens, water you from above, that is wrong. If you are going to ask the Lord to quench you, to water you, you have to open yourself to Him. By your opening, the indwelling Christ will well up and flow out (John 7:37-39a). The more He wells up, the more He will water you. You will be quenched from within, not from above. The well has been put into you. The spring of water is in us, in our spirit. This can be proved by John 4:24. The Lord is the Spirit, and if we are going to contact Him, we have to contact Him in our spirit. This means we have to learn to open ourselves. To exercise our spirit, we have to open ourselves.

Praise the Lord that the tree of life has been planted into us. What we need is to release Him. We must learn how to release the Spirit. Then we will enjoy Him as the air, water, food, light, and in a full way as the very tree of life. This is what we Christians need today. We should not just take this as a teaching. We have to put what we have heard into practice and always go to the Lord with such a realization that He is so much to us and lives within us.

We must exercise to open ourselves to contact Him. Then we will realize how real, how available, how fresh, and how refreshing He is to us. This enjoyment of the indwelling Christ as the tree of life will not only save us, deliver us, adjust us, regulate us, and correct us but will also transform us. We need to know Christ as the tree of life in the way of life. We need to know this living One in a living way so that the indwelling Christ as the inner life can transform our entire inward being.

Chapter Four

THE FATNESS OF THE LORD'S HOUSE

Scripture Reading: Psa. 23:6; 36:8-9; 27:4; 84:3, 10; 90:1; S. S. 2:3

GOD'S INTENTION FOR MAN TO ENJOY HIM AS FOOD

From the time that man was created, God first presented Himself to man as the tree of life in the form of food. When we partake of food, that food becomes a part of us. This is the very intention God has toward us, that we may take Him as food so that we can be mingled with Him to express Him in this universe. The first mentioning of something in the Scriptures is always a governing principle, a principle which governs all the Lord's dealings with us. The basic principle of the Lord's dealings with His people is that they would enjoy Him as their food, their life supply.

The Gospel of John tells us that one day this very God, who in the beginning presented Himself to man as food, was incarnated as a man. God in the form of a man presented Himself to man again as food, as the heavenly bread of life (6:35, 57), that man may partake of Him. In Genesis 2 at the beginning, God presented Himself as the tree of life to man in the form of food. In John 6 after His incarnation, He did the same thing. He presented Himself as the bread of life to man that man might partake of Him. In John 6:57 the Lord Jesus said, "He who eats Me shall also live because of Me."

Before man partook of the tree of life, Satan came in causing man to fall. After the fall, God still presented Himself to man, not as the plant life but as the animal life. This is because after the fall the shedding of blood is needed. After the fall, we need redemption, so in Genesis 3 a lamb was prepared and provided

by God for His fallen people (v. 21). Exodus 12 shows us that
with this redeeming lamb there is still the enjoyment of eating.
The shed blood of the lamb is for redemption, but the meat of
this lamb is for the redeemed ones to feed on (vv. 8-9). The lamb
brings us back to the tree of life. If man had not fallen, the plant
life would have been good enough for him to enjoy. But after the
fall, man needs not only the plant life, which is the nourishing,
generating life, but also the animal life, which is the redeeming life. The animal life involves the shedding of blood for
redemption, which can bring us back to the enjoyment of the
nourishing and generating life.

John tells us that the Lamb who takes away the sin of the
world is Christ Himself, who is the very God (1:1, 29). With
the eating of the Passover lamb there was also the unleavened
bread. The bread signifies nourishment. After you have been
redeemed, you have to feed on the Lord and be nourished by
the Lord. Along with the unleavened bread the children of
Israel were to eat bitter herbs. All these aspects of the Passover were for the enjoyment of the Lord's chosen people.

In the wilderness the children of Israel went on to enjoy
the heavenly manna, the living water out of the smitten rock,
and all the different offerings related to the tabernacle. The
book of Leviticus shows us the burnt offering, the meal offering, the peace offering, the sin offering, and the trespass
offering. All these offerings typify different aspects of Christ
for our enjoyment, and all of them except the burnt offering
were for eating. Christ becomes our enjoyment by and
through His redemption. In addition to these offerings there
are the wave offering and the heave offering. The wave offering typifies the resurrected Christ. Christ is the "waving One"
in resurrection. The heave offering typifies the ascended
Christ. He is the One who has been uplifted to the height
of the universe. The resurrected and ascended Christ has
become our enjoyment in the fullest way.

THE FULLNESS OF THE ENJOYMENT OF THE LORD

With all the offerings there is the tabernacle, and with the
tabernacle there is the priesthood. Eventually, the consummate
item in the Old Testament is the temple. Many do not have a

proper concept concerning the temple. We may have thought that the temple is only something for God, that it is merely the dwelling place of God. But we have to realize that the temple of God, the house of God, is not only something for God but also something for us. The temple is the fullest expression of God Himself being our enjoyment. God Himself as the temple becomes our dwelling place. This corresponds with the record of the Gospel of John. In John 15 the Lord tells us to abide in Him (v. 5), indicating that He is our dwelling place. In John 14 the Lord Jesus says that in His Father's house are many abodes and that He was going to prepare a place for us. John 14 and 15 both reveal that we are the Lord's abodes and that the Lord Himself is our abode. John 15:4a says, "Abide in Me and I in you." The Lord and we abide in one another mutually; this is a mutual abode.

God's intention is to make Himself our very enjoyment in many aspects that He may be thoroughly wrought into our being for us to be fully joined to Him and mingled with Him. The types, figures, and shadows of the Old Testament provide a clear picture that God's intention is to present Himself to us as our enjoyment. We need to learn how to enjoy Him. We need to enjoy Him as our life, our food, our drink, our light, our air, our dwelling place, and as our everything. Psalm 90:1 says, "Lord, thou hast been our dwelling place in all generations." The Lord is not only our life, food, drink, light, and air, but He is also our dwelling place. We have to dwell in Him. Our enjoyment of Him in so many aspects depends upon our realization that the Lord is the tree of life. The house of the Lord is the fullest expression of the tree of life and the fullest enjoyment of what the Lord is to us.

In Psalm 23 there are five steps of the experience of being shepherded by the Lord: the green pastures (v. 2), the paths of righteousness (v. 3), the valley of the shadow of death (v. 4), the battlefield (v. 5), and dwelling in the house of the Lord forever (v. 6). Verse 6 describes the fullness of the enjoyment of the Lord Himself—"Surely goodness and mercy shall follow me all the days of my life: and I will dwell in the house of the Lord for ever." The fullness of the enjoyment of the Lord is to enjoy Him as the dwelling place.

In the Gospel of John the Lord Jesus reveals Himself first as the tabernacle (1:14) and then as the temple (2:19-21). The Lord Jesus Himself is the temple, the house of the Lord. To dwell in the house of the Lord means to enjoy the Lord to the fullest extent. Psalm 23 shows us that we are the sheep under the Lord's shepherding to enjoy Him in many aspects as the green pastures, the paths of righteousness, and eventually as the dwelling place, the temple of God.

THE FATNESS OF THE LORD'S HOUSE

Psalm 36:8 says, "They shall be abundantly satisfied with the fatness of thy house; and thou shalt make them drink of the river of thy pleasures." We may say that we are satisfied with the Lord, but do we have some experience of being abundantly satisfied with the fatness of the Lord's house? What is the fatness of the Lord's house? It is the fountain of life, which is the Lord Himself. The fountain of life is in the house of the Lord. Psalm 36:9 says, "For with thee is the fountain of life: in thy light shall we see light." With this fountain of life there is the light. This absolutely corresponds with John 1:4: "In Him was life, and the life was the light of men." The fatness of the Lord's house is the fountain of life with the source of light. Whenever you enjoy the Lord Jesus as your life, you sense that you are enlightened.

In the holy place of the tabernacle the serving priest first went to the showbread table, typifying the Lord as the bread of life, the life supply, to us. Then he would proceed to the lampstand, which signifies Christ as the light of life (John 8:12). When we enjoy the Lord as life, we enjoy the light of life and sense something within us shining. The more you enjoy the Lord as life, the more you sense that you are filled with light and enlightened within. From the lampstand the priest then proceeded to the incense altar to burn the incense. This typifies our prayer to the Lord ascending as a sweet savor unto Him. This shows us the fatness of the Lord's house which comes from the experience of the fountain of life and the source of light.

Whenever you experience the Lord in such a way as life and as light and as the sweet savor of incense in your prayer to God, you will immediately sense the need of the building up of the Body, of the Lord's house, of the corporate church life. The more you enjoy Christ as life, the more you will desire, hunger, and thirst for the church life. The more you enjoy the Lord, the more you will sense the need to fellowship with others. When you get into the church life, into the Lord's house, the house of the Lord will bring you back to all the many experiences of Christ and will enrich and strengthen these experiences. Then you will be satisfied abundantly with the fatness of the house of the Lord. You will see that the fountain of life and the source of light are in the house of the Lord. If you are not in the house of the Lord, it is possible for you to have a foretaste of the fountain of life and the source of light, and this foretaste will bring you and cause you to get into the church life. When you get into the church life, into the house of the Lord, you will say, "Here is the place where there is the fountain of life and the source of light." You will have a real sense of the sweetness, the fatness, of the Lord's house.

REDEEMING OUR TIME
BY REMAINING IN THE LORD'S HOUSE

In Psalm 27:4 David said, "One thing have I desired of the Lord, that will I seek after; that I may dwell in the house of the Lord all the days of my life, to behold the beauty of the Lord, and to inquire in his temple." The only thing that David was seeking was to dwell in the Lord's house for his entire life. In Psalm 84:10 the psalmist said, "For a day in thy courts is better than a thousand. I had rather be a doorkeeper in the house of my God, than to dwell in the tents of wickedness." The best way to redeem our time is to keep ourselves in the courts of the Lord. One day there is better than a thousand days. Some people may criticize you by saying that you are wasting your time, but actually you are not wasting your time. You are gaining your time one thousand fold by remaining in the Lord's house in the enjoyment of the Lord.

THE MINGLING OF DIVINITY WITH HUMANITY

The Lord's house in the Old Testament was first the

tabernacle and then the temple. In the tabernacle and the
temple there were two main materials—acacia wood and
gold. The wood was overlaid with gold and united, knit
together, by the gold. Forty-eight standing boards of acacia
wood formed the main part of the tabernacle. All of these
forty-eight boards were overlaid with gold. There were
golden rings on each board which served to unite the boards
(Exo. 26:24). In addition there were bars made of acacia
wood overlaid with gold running through the boards to con-
nect them (26:26-29). The acacia wood signifies the human
nature, and the gold signifies the divine nature. The divine
nature and the human nature have to be built up together
and mingled together as one. Thus, the dwelling place of the
Lord, the temple of the Lord, is the mingling of divinity with
humanity.

The first mention of the house of God is in Genesis 28 with
Jacob. Jacob had a dream of a ladder set up on the earth with
the angels of God ascending and descending on it (v. 12).
When Jacob awoke he said, "This is none other but the house
of God, and this is the gate of heaven" (v. 17). Verse 18 says,
"And Jacob rose up early in the morning, and took the stone
that he had put for his pillows, and set it up for a pillar, and
poured oil upon the top of it." Jacob then called this place
Bethel, which means the house of God (v. 19). The stone with
oil poured upon it is Bethel, the temple of God, the house of
God. We are the stone, and God is the oil. Thus, in this picture we again see the principle of the mingling of God with
man. The house of God, the temple of God, is the mingling of
divinity with humanity.

When God was incarnated, the divine nature was mingled
with the human nature. Jesus, the incarnated God, was the
mingling of the divine nature with the human nature, and
He told us that He was the temple (John 2:20-22). Through the
Lord's death and resurrection, this temple was enlarged to
become the church, the Body of Christ (1 Cor. 3:16). The church
as the temple of God is the mingling of God with man in a corporate way. There was not just one board in the tabernacle but
forty-eight boards overlaid with gold. This mingling of God with
man is the mutual abode, the dwelling place of God and the

dwelling place of His seeking ones. God's seeking ones are His abode, and He is their abode. Through the death and resurrection of Christ, the mingling of God with His chosen and redeemed people to produce the mutual abode has been accomplished.

THE ENJOYMENT AND EXPERIENCE OF CHRIST

Today's religious system has distracted us from the enjoyment of Christ. Religion has teachings, rules, and rituals for people to worship God, to serve God. The teachings in religion deal with how to adjust a person's character and how to improve his behavior. In today's Christianity there are many teachings and gifts, but the sad thing is that the central thought of God revealed in the Scriptures has been greatly missed and even lost. The central thought of God is that God wants to be our enjoyment. We have to partake of Him and enjoy Him, not just to know Him with a certain amount of objective knowledge but to know Him in our subjective experience. We have to taste Him as David charged us to do in Psalm 34:8—"O taste and see that the Lord is good." In Psalm 36 we are told that we need to be abundantly satisfied with the fatness of the Lord's house, enjoying the fountain of life in the Lord's light. This describes the enjoyment of the Lord and the experience of the Lord Himself. It is not enough to have some objective knowledge about the Lord and to learn many doctrines and teachings concerning the Lord. We must experience the Lord and taste the Lord.

The seeking one in Song of Songs said, "As the apple tree among the trees of the wood, so is my beloved among the sons. I sat down under his shadow with great delight, and his fruit was sweet to my taste" (2:3). This indicates how precious the Lord is to the seeking one. He is like an apple tree providing the seeking one with shade and rich fruit. We can rest under His shadow and enjoy His fruit, which are all His riches for our enjoyment. The apple tree is not for the scientific study of the seeking one but for her to rest under its shadow and enjoy the fruit. We need to experience and enjoy the Lord in such a way.

For many years I have been taught, helped, and even strengthened to enjoy the Lord in such a way. This is why we should not focus on the doctrines, the teachings, and the gifts, but we should focus our entire being on the Lord Himself. We should learn to enjoy Him, to contact Him, to eat Him, to partake of Him. The Lord said, "He who eats Me shall also live because of Me" (John 6:57). We must learn to know the Lord in such an experiential way, day by day tasting Him and being satisfied with Him. We need to be satisfied with the fatness of His house, saturated and permeated with His sweetness.

THE ISSUE OF OUR ENJOYMENT OF THE LORD

If we enjoy the Lord in this way, this enjoyment will create a deep hunger within us for the Lord's heart's desire, His dwelling place. This enjoyment will stir us up to pray, "Lord, bring me fully into the experience of the church life. Keep me in Your courts and in Your house all the days of my life." The enjoyment of the Lord will bring you into the church life, and the church life will cause you to enjoy Him even more as the fountain of life and the source of light. Sometimes people would ask us where we received all our light from. They wondered what books we studied to get this light from the Word. Actually the light we have received is from the living Lord Himself in the church. In the church the Bible is an open book. The church is typified by the tabernacle. Within the tabernacle is the showbread table which is the source, the fountain, of life, and the lampstand, which is the source of light. Life and light are both in the house of the Lord, in the church, God's building. This life and light are inexhaustible in the church. In the Lord's house the light even floods in, as the psalmist said, "In thy light shall we see light" (Psa. 36:9).

The issue of the enjoyment of the tree of life is the tabernacle, the house of the Lord. If we enjoy Him in such a living and real way as the tree of life, we will have the tabernacle and we will be in the house of the Lord. At that time we will be able to say that we are satisfied with the fatness of the house of the Lord. We will enjoy Him as the fountain of life and the source of light. We will only desire to dwell in His house all the days of our life and will have a full realization that one day in His courts is better than a thousand. We will be like the sparrow who has found a house and the swallow who has found a nest for her young in the altars of the house (Psa. 84:3). The church life will be our resting place and a nest to take care of the younger ones whom we have brought to the Lord. Thank and praise the Lord for the fatness of His house.

CHAPTER FIVE

THE FRUIT OF THE TREE OF LIFE

Scripture Reading: John 6:35, 57, 63; 7:37; 8:12; 9:5; 11:25; 1 Cor. 15:45

CHRIST AS THE TREE OF LIFE
AND THE LAMB OF GOD

The first picture in the entire Bible is that God offered Himself to man as the tree of life in the form of food, that man may take Him in, eat Him, and have Him as his life. After this, man fell. But immediately after the fall of man, God provided him a lamb. If you read the Scriptures with a heavenly view, you will see who this lamb is. After the fall of man, God not only provided a lamb for fallen man but also offered a lamb for him (Gen. 3:21; 4:4). Adam became fallen, yet due to his enjoyment of the lamb as his covering, his clothing, he could still live. Abel, Noah, Abraham, Isaac, Jacob, and all of their descendants, the sons of Israel, also enjoyed the lamb (Gen. 4:4; 8:20; 12:7; 26:25; 35:7; Exo. 12:3-10).

The Passover feast was a new beginning for the children of Israel (Exo. 12:2). Their history began with a lamb. The lamb was slain, the blood was shed for redemption (12:3, 7; 13:13, 15), and the meat of the lamb was eaten (12:8-10). In the Bible, first there is the tree of life and then the lamb. In John 1:29, John the Baptist declared that Christ was the Lamb of God. Christ as the Lamb of God is the Word, who is God incarnated to be a man (vv. 1, 14). Christ is the complete God and the perfect man, the God-man.

After creation, before the fall of man, God offered Himself to man as the tree of life (Gen. 2:9, 16). After the fall of man, God offered Himself as a lamb (3:21; 4:4) because there was the need of redemption. With the tree of life before the fall, there was no need of redemption because there was no sin. With the fall sin came in (Rom. 5:12); thus, redemption is required. After the fall, the tree of life alone is not sufficient to meet man's need. After the fall man needs redemption (Heb. 9:22) and with the lamb, there is redemption. Before the fall, God ordained that man should eat only vegetables (Gen. 1:29), not animals. After the fall and its development, God changed His ordination, giving man not only vegetables but also animals to eat (9:3).

The tree of life is a matter of nourishment, and the lamb is a matter of redemption. Yet even with the lamb there is something for nourishment. The Lord's word in John 6 is difficult for many readers to understand. Even many of the Lord's disciples at that time stumbled at His word. They said, "This is a hard word; who can hear it?" (v. 60b). The Lord said that He was the bread of life (v. 35) and that His blood was true drink (v. 55). It is not possible for physical bread to have blood. Yet the Lord Jesus as the bread of life said, "My flesh is true food, and My blood is true drink" (v. 55). The Lord Jesus as the bread of life indicated that He was a continuation of the tree of life for man's nourishment. The blood and the flesh are two items indicating that Christ is the Lamb of God (1:29).

After the fall of man, if Christ were not the Lamb, He could never be the bread. Without redemption, He could never be our nourishment. Redemption is not the goal, the aim, but the procedure to reach the goal. The Lord Jesus shed His blood for redemption so that we might eat His flesh for our nourishment. In a similar way, the Passover lamb was slain, the blood of the lamb was sprinkled upon the doors, and in the house under the covering of the sprinkled blood, the children of Israel rested and enjoyed the meat of the lamb (Exo. 12:3-11).

CHRIST AS THE TEMPLE

First, God presented Himself as the tree of life. Then after the fall, God presented Himself as the lamb and through the lamb His redeemed people began to enjoy God. The Old Testament saints continued to enjoy God in many aspects, and eventually, they enjoyed God to the fullest extent as the temple. At the end of the Old Testament the temple is the product of the enjoyment of God and is the fullest enjoyment of God. In the New Testament Jesus came as the very God. The Gospel of John says, "In the beginning was the Word...and the Word was God" (1:1). This very God one day was incarnated as a man to be a God-man, who is the Lamb of God (v. 29). In John 2, the Lord Jesus, the God-man, told us that He was the temple (vv. 19-21). His forerunner, John the Baptist, declared that He was the Lamb, and the Lord Himself declared that He was the temple. His forerunner told us the first item and Jesus Himself told us the last item. In between these two items, there are many items of Christ in the Gospel of John.

THE ITEMS OF CHRIST IN THE GOSPEL OF JOHN FOR OUR ENJOYMENT

In John 1 He is the Word who is God (1:1). In Him was life, and this life is the light of men (v. 4). He is the One who is received by His believers and gives them the authority to be the children of God (v. 12). He is the One incarnated as a man, the Word who became flesh who is full of grace and reality (v. 14). He is the One who is declared and testified to us to be the very Lamb of God (v. 29). Ultimately, He is the heavenly ladder who joins the earth to the heaven and who brings heaven to the earth (v. 51).

In John 2, He is not only the temple (vv. 19, 21) but also the wine (v. 10). Wine is a real enjoyment. In this portion of the word, wine, the life-juice of the grape, signifies life. Water signifies death (Gen. 1:2, 6; Exo. 14:21; Matt. 3:16a). The Lord changed water into wine, which means that the Lord swallowed up death, changing death into life (v. 9).

In John 3 there are several items of Christ for our enjoyment. First, Christ is the brass serpent. As Moses lifted up the brass serpent on the pole, even so Christ as the Son of Man was lifted up on the cross. God told Moses to lift up a brass serpent on behalf of the children of Israel for God's judgment. Whoever looked upon the brass serpent would live. In John 3:14, the Lord Jesus applied this type to Himself, showing that He was in "the likeness of the flesh of sin" (Rom. 8:3). The brass serpent had the likeness, the form, of the serpent, but without the poison. Christ was made in "the likeness of the flesh of sin," but He had no participation in the sin of the flesh (2 Cor. 5:21; Heb. 4:15). After the serpent in chapter three, there is Christ as the bridegroom (v. 29).

In chapter four, there is not only the living water, but also a well (v. 14). This well, which replaces Jacob's well (v. 6), is the eternal well, the heavenly well, and within this well, there is the living water (vv. 11, 14). The living water is the content of the well. Also in chapter four, there is the harvest (v. 35). In chapter five, the Lord Jesus is the very substitution, the replacement, for any kind of religion. In this chapter the law-keeping religion, the Jewish religion with its pool and angels, is replaced by the Lord Jesus as the substitution of all things. He is much better than the angels (Heb. 1:4). He is the substitution for the law-keeping of any kind of religion. If we have Him, we do not need religion.

In chapter six, there is Christ as the bread of life. Included in the bread of life is the Lamb with the blood to shed and the meat for eating (John 6:35; 1:29; 6:51 and note 51[4]—Recovery Version). In chapter seven, the Spirit is the rivers of living water (vv. 38-39 and note 38[4]—Recovery Version). In chapter eight, there is Christ as the great "I Am." This title, "I Am," is mentioned at least three times in this chapter: 1) "Unless you believe that I am, you shall die in your sins" (v. 24); 2) "When you lift up the Son of Man, then you will know that I am" (v. 28); and 3) "Before Abraham came into being, I am" (v. 58). "I Am" indicates that Christ is all-inclusive. He is whatever we need. He is like a blank, endorsed check. As the I Am, He is whatever you need. If you need healing, "I Am" is healing. If you need life, "I Am" is life. If you need power, "I Am" is power. If you need light, "I Am" is light. What you need, He is. He is I am that I am, the great I Am (Exo. 3:14). How rich is the Gospel of John!

In chapter nine, Christ is the light of the world (v. 5). Chapter ten reveals that Christ is the shepherd (v. 11; Psa. 23:1) and the door (vv. 2, 9). This door in chapter ten is not only for God's elect to enter, but also for His people to come out. It is not a door for entering heaven, it is a door to come out of the bondage of the law. We all must come out of the fold. Who is the door for us to come out? Christ is the door. Christ is the door, not only for God's elect to enter into the custody of the law, as did Moses, David, Isaiah, Jeremiah, and others, in the Old Testament time before Christ came; but also for God's chosen people, such as Peter, John, James, Paul, and others to come out of the fold of the law after Christ came. Thus, the Lord indicates here that He is the door not only for God's chosen people to go in, but also for God's chosen people to go out.

Christ is not only the door but also the pasture (10:9). Pasture signifies Christ as the feeding place for the sheep. When the pasture is not available in the winter time or in the night, the sheep must be kept in the fold. When the pasture is ready, there is no further need for the sheep to remain in the fold. To be kept in the fold is transitory and temporary. To be in the pasture to enjoy its riches is final and permanent. Before Christ came, the law was a ward, and to be under the law was transitory. Now, since Christ has come, all God's people must come out of the law and come into Him to enjoy Him as their pasture (Gal. 3:23-25; 4:3-5). This should be final and permanent. Christ is our shepherd, the door for us to leave the fold of the law, and the pasture, the feeding place, after we leave the fold. Ultimately, in chapter ten He tells us that He is one with the Father (v. 30), so He is the Father (14:9; Isa. 9:6).

In chapter eleven, Christ is resurrection (v. 25). He is not only life, but resurrection. Resurrection is life which has been tested even with death. The strongest thing in the whole universe besides God is death, yet even death cannot hold the resurrection life. Christ is the resurrection and the life.

In chapter twelve, Christ is the grain of wheat (v. 24). If a grain of wheat is sown into the earth, it dies and then grows up to become many grains. His death released the divine life concealed within Him (1:4). In chapter thirteen is the significance of the Lord washing the disciples' feet (v. 5). This is like the laver in the outer court of the tabernacle (Exo. 30:18-21), which washed the priests from earthly defilement. The washing of feet in chapter thirteen indicates that until this chapter, the things are still only in the outer court and not yet in the holy place or in the Holy of Holies. It is not until chapter fourteen, following the experience of the laver, that we enter into the holy place.

In chapter fourteen, Christ is the Father (vv. 9-11) and the Spirit (vv. 16-18). The Lord Jesus is the embodiment and expression of the Father, and as the Spirit, the Son is revealed and realized. The Father is His fullness, and all the fullness of the Godhead dwells in Him bodily (Col. 2:9). The Father as the fullness and the reality dwells in the Son, and the Son is now the Spirit. The Spirit is the transmission of the Triune God, as revealed in 2 Corinthians 13:14 which says, "The grace of the Lord Jesus Christ, and the love of God, and the fellowship of the Holy Spirit be with you all." The fellowship of the Spirit is the Spirit Himself as the transmission of the grace of the Lord with the love of God for our participation.

In chapter fifteen, Christ is the great, universal vine. In chapter sixteen are the Spirit (vv. 7, 13-15) and the newborn child (v. 21). Christ is this newborn child. He is the firstborn of the dead (Col. 1:18), the firstborn of the newborn ones. He is the firstborn Son of God brought forth in resurrection (Acts 13:33; Heb. 1:5; Rom. 1:4).

The prayer of the Lord concerning the divine oneness in chapter seventeen is fully answered and realized in the New Jerusalem. John 17:23 says, "I in them, and You in Me, that they may be perfected into one." The believers are to be perfected into one in the Triune God that they might be perfect. The universal building, the mingling of the Triune God with all the believers, is the New Jerusalem, which is the answer to the prayer of John 17. In the New Jerusalem, all the believers will be perfected into one in the Triune God. In chapter eighteen, Christ is the real Lamb who was judged, the One who bore the universal judgment. He was the real Passover Lamb examined for four days before He was put to death (See Mark 12:37 and note 37[1]—Recovery Version; Exo. 12:3-6).

In chapter nineteen is the cross with the blood and the water (vv. 17, 34), and in chapter twenty is the breath of life. The Lord Jesus breathed into the disciples and said, "Receive the Holy Spirit" (v. 22). In chapter twenty-one there are fish

and lambs. With the fish there is also bread for eating
(vv. 9, 13). There is no need for us to fish; the Lord has the fish
already (vv. 5, 9 and note 9[1]—Recovery Version). After our sat-
isfaction, we have to take care of the little lambs (vv. 15-17).
These are the items of Christ as God's embodiment in the
Gospel of John for us to enjoy.

THE ULTIMATE CONSUMMATION
OF OUR ENJOYMENT OF GOD

The whole Scripture reveals nothing but God, the Triune
God, the Father in the Son as the Spirit. Such a wonderful
Triune God offered Himself to us as our enjoyment in many
items. This enjoyment starts with the Lamb and consummates
in its fullest way with the temple. Eventually, the temple is
enlarged into a city, the New Jerusalem, where God Himself
is the temple (Rev. 21:22). In 1 Samuel (1:9; 3:3), the tabernacle
in Shiloh was called the temple before the temple was built by
Solomon. Thus, the tabernacle is the temple. The New Jerusalem is called the tabernacle of God (Rev. 21:3). We are God's
tabernacle for God to dwell in, and He is our temple for us to
dwell in. This city is a mutual abode for God and His chosen
and redeemed people. The New Jerusalem is the climax of our
enjoyment of the Triune God where we will enjoy God in the
fullest way.

We have to see the heavenly vision that God is the tree of
life for us to enjoy. All of the items of what Christ is in John
are the outcome, the outflowing, of the tree of life. If we read
the Scriptures again to find out what are the aspects, the
items, of God being our enjoyment, the Bible will become a
new book to us. It will become a book of life instead of a book of
knowledge. Many take the Bible as a book of knowledge, but
we have to change our realization of this book. The Bible is a
book of life. This wonderful Triune God is our enjoyment in
many aspects revealed in the Scriptures.

In the New Jerusalem there is still the Lamb (Rev. 22:1).
The Lamb is the center of the city and its temple (21:22). In the
new heaven and new earth the temple of God will be enlarged
into a city. Again we see the Lamb and the temple. The Lamb
is the lamp, and within Him is God as the light. The Lamb as

the lamp shines with God as the light to illumine the city with the glory of God, the expression of the divine light. God as light in Christ shines as life to flow out as the living water, the Spirit. On both sides of the water of life, there is the tree of life (Rev. 22:2), which is the nourishment, the supply of life, to all the redeemed ones. The Father is the very source as the light (1 John 1:5; Rev. 22:5), the One who dwells in unapproachable light (1 Tim. 6:16). The Holy Spirit is signified by the flow of the living water, the water of life (John 7:38-39). Along the flow of the living water is the tree of life which signifies Christ the Son (John 1:4; 15:1). Thus, the Triune God is the very content of this universal building and is enjoyed by His redeemed ones in the fullest way. The book of Genesis shows us the source of the tree of life, and the book of Revelation gives us the consummation. In between these two ends is the Gospel of John. The major items mentioned in the two ends of the Bible, such as the Lamb, the temple, and the tree of life, are also mentioned in the Gospel of John (1:29; 2:19, 21; 15:1).

THE WAY TO ENJOY CHRIST

The vital point is that we need to enjoy this wonderful One as so many items. God the Father is in the Son (John 14:10, 11) and God the Son is the Spirit (2 Cor. 3:17; 1 Cor. 15:45b). We must realize that not only is God Himself Spirit (John 4:24), but that all of what God is, what He has attained, and what He has accomplished, has been wrought into the Spirit. After the resurrection and ascension of Christ, many things were accomplished by God; thus, God has many attainments. He has accomplished creation, incarnation, human living, crucifixion, resurrection, and ascension. All of what He is and has, all of what He has attained and accomplished, has been put into this one Spirit.

Now He is this wonderful and profound Spirit, which is likened to breath (John 20:22). In John 20, everything concerning the promise of the Holy Spirit as the Comforter was accomplished, so the Lord Jesus came to the disciples, breathed on them, and said to them, "Receive the Holy Spirit" (v. 22). The all-inclusive, profound Holy Spirit is like the breath. All of what God is, all of what God has accomplished, and all of what God has attained is in this Spirit, this breath. The Spirit is like the air, so applicable, available, near, and dear. Because He is the air, Romans 10:13 says, "Whoever calls upon the name of the Lord shall be saved." Therefore, the unbelievers who are going to receive Christ do not need to go to heaven to bring Christ down (v. 6) or go to the abyss to bring Christ up (v. 7). The reason is that Christ, the living Word, is near them, in their mouth and even in their heart (v. 8). If they would exercise their mouth to call, "Lord Jesus," Christ as the all-inclusive breath would come into them.

According to the Gospel of John, this wonderful divine Spirit came into our human spirit (John 3:6) at the time we received Him. Thus, 1 Corinthians 6:17 says, "He who is joined to the Lord is one spirit," and Romans 8:16 says, "The Spirit Himself witnesses with our spirit." Since God is Spirit (John 4:24) and He is now in our spirit (2 Tim. 4:22) we must worship Him in spirit and in reality.

Christ is in us as so many items! The first item is the Lamb, the One who redeems us. The last item is the building, the temple, which is enlarged to be a city. However, the key to our experience of Christ is that He is the Spirit in us. John 4 tells us that the spring of water is in the one who drinks the water given by the Lord. John 7 tells us that rivers of living water will flow out of the innermost being of the person who believes in the Lord Jesus (v. 39). Many rivers of living water will flow out from within our spirit, our innermost being. I once thought that the Lord would flow water into me, but the Lord wells up within us and flows out of us because He is in us already. There is little need for Him to come in, but there is much need for Him to come out, to flow out. However, why can He not flow out? You and I are the problem. Therefore, there is the need for us to open ourselves to the Lord.

The divine Spirit is within us energizing, empowering, strengthening, and even disturbing us. Through Christ's redemption, by His blood, we have been cleansed and purged to fit His purpose of indwelling us. He is now dwelling within our spirit. All that the Triune God is and all that He has attained and accomplished is within our spirit. Now we must learn to open ourselves to Him, realizing that He is everything within us. We can never exhaust what He is within us. He is the great I Am (John 8:24, 28, 58). Whatever we need, He is.

There is no need for a husband to ask, "Lord, help me to deal with my dear wife. I do not know how to deal with her." Just learn to open yourself to Him saying, "Lord, I just open myself to You. Once again, here is a chance for me to open myself to You." Sometimes it is difficult for the Lord to get you to open from the depths of your being. Therefore, the Lord gives you the right wife to help you to open yourself to the Lord. He is the great I Am. He is the answer. He will meet your need. If you open to Him, you will know how to deal with your wife, not in the way of mere mental knowledge, but according to the life within. From within, you will know how to deal with your wife in a proper way, in a divine way, in a heavenly way, in a way that will bring growth in the Lord to you.

Because the Lord is within, you must learn to open yourself to Him. Whenever you open yourself to Him, He will flow out. We have frustrated and even imprisoned the Lord within us so much. We pay attention to things other than the Lord Himself. You may pray, "Lord, correct my dear wife, change her attitude, and tell her that she is wrong." This is the wrong way to pray. In the Lord's sovereignty, a man's wife can help him to open himself to the Lord. When you open yourself to the Lord, the rivers of living water, such as the river of life, the river of love, the river of wisdom, the river of humility, the river of mercy, and the river of patience, will flow from within you to water you and others. This is the issue of the enjoyment of the tree of life.

In Genesis 2 there is the tree of life with the flow of a river (vv. 9-10). When we really enjoy the Lord as the tree of life, there will be an issue. Something will flow out of us to minister something of the Lord Himself to others. This flow will quench others' thirst, feed others, enlighten others, or strengthen others. This is the proper way for us to live on this earth as the testimony of Jesus. This is what the Lord needs today. He does not need a religion with various kinds of teachings, practices, and gifts; rather, He needs this flow of life from within us. We need to realize what He is and where He is. He is such a wonderful, rich, all-inclusive Spirit, and He is in our spirit. He is waiting for us to open ourselves to Him. Do not trust in yourself and do not endeavor to do anything by your own effort. There is only one lesson for us to learn: to open ourselves to the Lord. Then He will come out; He will spring up from within us. As a result, we will have rivers of living water flowing out of us all the time. This is the issue, the result, of the enjoyment of God as the all-inclusive tree of life.

CHAPTER SIX

THE TREE OF LIFE FOR TRANSFORMATION

Scripture Reading: Lev. 2:7-10; 7:14-15

OUR NEED TO UNDERSTAND THE BIBLE
WITH DIVINE INSIGHT IN AN INNER AND LIVING WAY

The entire sixty-six books of the Bible are the Holy Spirit's revelation (John 16:13) and are the speaking from God by men borne by the Holy Spirit (2 Pet. 1:21). The entire Bible was inspired by the one Spirit and was written with a definite purpose to show us God's heart's desire. To acquire the divine insight into the Bible in its entirety is not an easy task. Matthew 22 records that one day the Sadducees came to question the Lord concerning the matter of resurrection. They did not believe that there was a resurrection. The Lord told them that they did not know the Scriptures nor the power of God (v. 29) and He answered them in this way, "But concerning the resurrection of the dead, have you not read that which was spoken to you by God, saying, I am the God of Abraham, and the God of Isaac, and the God of Jacob? He is not the God of the dead, but of the living" (vv. 31-32).

As God is the God of the living and is called the God of Abraham, Isaac, and Jacob, so the dead Abraham, Isaac, and Jacob will be resurrected. This is the way the Lord Jesus handled the Scriptures—not only by the letter but by the life and power implied within them. From the divine title of God as the God of Abraham, Isaac, and Jacob, the Lord Jesus saw the truth, the fact, of resurrection. It is not so easy to understand the Bible in such an inner way and in such a living way. Apparently there is nothing to see in this title, but in such a title there is the truth of resurrection because God could not be the God of a dead person. If God is the God of Abraham, who has died, Abraham will be resurrected because He is not the God of the dead but of the living.

EATING THE TREE OF LIFE

The Lord needs to bring us into the understanding of the Scriptures in an inner and living way to see what is on His heart. After the creation of man, God presented Himself to man as the tree of life for man to eat. The only thing God desired man to do was to feed on Him, to partake of Him as the tree of life. He wanted man to take Him in as life, to learn how to live, how to exist, by the tree of life. Without eating, a person cannot exist. You may have life, but your life cannot last without your eating. In presenting Himself to man as the tree of life, God's intention was for man to learn how to live by depending on God, by taking God as his daily supply and as his entire supply. Most of us eat three meals a day for our life supply. We live, exist, by eating. God did not command man to do anything but to eat. Man has to take care of his eating. If he eats in a right way, he will be right. If he eats in a wrong way, he will be wrong. If you eat something of life, you will have life. If you eat something of death, you will have death. The Christian life is not merely a matter of doing or working, but a matter of partaking of God as the tree of life. This point was clearly made by the Lord Jesus in John 6 where He said that He was the bread of life (v. 35) and that the one who ate Him would live because of Him (v. 57).

THE LAMB OF GOD

The tree of life was the first item presented by God to man, but after man's fall God made coats of skins of the sacrifice for Adam and his wife and clothed them. The coats fully covered them, which means that God justified them (Gen. 3:21). To be justified means to be covered with the righteousness of God, which is Christ Himself. In order to make coats of the skins of the lambs, God probably killed the lambs in the presence of Adam and Eve. Their putting on of the coats of skins was based upon the shedding of the blood of the sacrifice, for the sacrificial lamb became a substitute for sinful man. Before the fall in Genesis 2 is the tree of life presented to man by God. After the fall in Genesis 3 is the lamb, the sacrifice, offered to man by God. The tree of life in Genesis 2 changed to a lamb in Genesis 3. The tree of life is Christ, and the lamb is Christ. These two items are one. Because of the fall the tree of life had to become the lamb.

In John 6 the Lord Jesus tells us that He is the bread of life. The bread of life equals the tree of life. Both of these items are of the plant life, the vegetable life. But in the same chapter where the Lord Jesus talks about eating Him as the bread of life, He also says, "For My flesh is true food, and My blood is true drink" (v. 55). In a physical sense bread cannot have blood. But according to the spiritual reality, the bread of life includes the blood. This is because the bread of life, without the blood, could never be eaten by us. The tree of life was closed to us by the fall, but it is opened to us by the Lamb with His redeeming blood.

After the fall, the Lamb is the first item of our enjoyment of God in both the Old and New Testaments. All the other items of the enjoyment of the Lord follow and come out of this first item. Even in eternity in the New Jerusalem, Christ will still be the eternal Lamb of God (Rev. 21:22; 22:1). In Revelation the Lamb is the lamp, and within the lamp is God as the light (21:23). Whatever God is as our portion for our enjoyment is in the Lamb, who is the lamp. We must enjoy Him first as the Lamb of God. After the presentation of the tree of life to man, from Genesis 3 through Exodus 12 there is the Lamb of God for the enjoyment of His chosen people.

THE SECRET OF TURNING FROM THE OUTER COURT INTO THE HOLY PLACE

Now we have to go on to see something more, something richer, something deeper, and something higher than enjoying Christ as the Lamb of God. After the book of Exodus is the book of Leviticus with all the offerings. All the offerings are based on two things—on the tree of life, the vegetable life, and on the lamb, the animal life. All the offerings are composed of these two kinds of lives. The burnt offering is of the animal life but the meal offering is of the vegetable life (Lev. 2:7-10).

The animal life is for redeeming, and the vegetable life is for generating, for nourishing. All of the offerings such as the sin offering, the trespass offering, the burnt offering, the meal offering, and the peace offering, were enjoyed in the outer court of the tabernacle. These offerings are types of Christ as the unique offering. In the holy place there were the show-bread table with the showbread, the lampstand with the light, and the golden incense altar with the incense. The table, the stand, and the altar are Christ, and the showbread, the light, and the incense are Christ. All the offerings are Christ, all the furniture in the holy place is Christ, and all the items related to the furniture are Christ.

How can we turn ourselves from the experience of Christ as all the offerings to the experience of Christ as all the furniture in the holy place with all the related items? In other words, how can we have a turn from the experience of Christ in the outer court to the experience of Christ in the holy place? The way to have this turn is by eating. Eating is the secret. In the outer court, the priest does not eat the offerings first. The offerings are slain and presented to God first. The blood of the offerings typifies the redeeming aspect of Christ. After redemption, we have to eat. The turning point is the eating. Eating is the secret which turns us from the outer court into the holy place. In the outer court, the priests first enjoyed all the offerings in the aspect of Christ as their righteousness. Then they went on to enjoy the offerings by eating (Lev. 7:14-15). After redemption is realized, we must go on to eat. Our eating of the offerings ushers us into the holy place. When we get into the holy place, the first item is the show-bread for our eating. If you do not know how to feed on the Lord Jesus, you are a Christian merely in the outer court. When you see the vision of eating the Lord and begin to feed on the Lord, this feeding turns you from the outer court into the holy place.

BROUGHT OUT OF EGYPT BY EATING

In Exodus 12, the children of Israel enjoyed the shedding of the blood of the Passover lamb to fulfill the righteous requirement of God. Following that they were instructed to eat the meat of the lamb. By this eating they were energized, strengthened, supplied, and enabled to get out of Egypt. Their eating of the lamb was for moving out of Egypt. Eating brings us out of Egypt, the outer court, into the wilderness, the holy place. In the wilderness the children of Israel enjoyed manna daily and in the holy place the priest enjoyed the showbread. The children of Israel were wandering in the wilderness, but they were living by heavenly food.

EATING THE FATTENED CALF WITHIN THE FATHER'S HOUSE

In Luke 15 the Lord Jesus told a parable of a loving father and a prodigal son. After the son came back, the father clothed him with the best robe and put a ring on his hand and sandals on his feet (v. 22). The father ran to receive the returning sinner and clothed him outside the house. Before being dressed, the prodigal son was a beggar and not worthy of coming into the father's house. Although the son had been approved by the father and clothed properly, he was still hungry. Thus, the father ordered his servants to bring the fattened calf and slaughter it for his returning son to eat (v. 23). Then they proceeded to feast on the fattened calf within the father's house. The robe is Christ as our righteousness to dress us, to clothe us, according to God's righteous requirements that we may be justified in the eyes of God (Jer. 23:6; 1 Cor. 1:30; Phil. 3:9). The fattened calf signifies the rich Christ (Eph. 3:8) killed on the cross for the believers' enjoyment.

Many Christians treasure the fact that Christ is their righteousness, but they neglect the eating of Christ for their inward enjoyment. God used Martin Luther to recover the truth concerning justification by faith with Christ as our righteousness. But the eating of Christ for our enjoyment still must be fully recovered among God's children. The fulfillment of God's purpose mostly depends upon the eating of Christ. Christ is our outward, objective righteousness so that we can feast on Him inwardly and subjectively.

After eating the fattened calf and being filled up, the son could do something to please the father. Our doing is not merely something out of the righteousness but out of the eating. If the

father in Luke 15 had only dressed the son up and then told
him to do something for him, he would not have had the
strength. The son was dressed nicely and cleansed thoroughly,
but he was hungry and empty within. He had no energy, no
power, no strength, and no filling up. After we have been
brought to the table to feed on Christ as our feast, we will be so
active, waiting for the Father's command. We will have the
strength, the energy, and the supply of life to carry out the
Father's will.

We value the objective side of the Lord's redemption, our
justification through His precious blood. But our redemption
and justification is so that we can eat Christ, enjoy Christ.
The father of the prodigal son dressed him up outside the
door for him to come in and feast at the table where they
could eat and be merry. All of us need to be those feasting on
the Lord to enjoy Him. We may have been saved through the
Lord's redemption, but how much have we been feasting on
the Lord? In our experience are we outside the door of the
Father's house or inside the door feasting on Christ with all
His riches? You may be outside the door clothed with the best
robe, with a ring on your hand and sandals on your feet, but
how are you within? Are you satisfied and filled up or empty?
We all need to eat the Lord to be filled with Him. When we
eat Him, we are enjoying Him as the tree of life. Christ as the
Lamb of God enables us to be justified by faith so that we can
be brought back to the enjoyment of Christ as the tree of life.

EATING CHRIST TO BE TRANSFORMED
INTO PRECIOUS MATERIALS FOR GOD'S BUILDING

By eating and enjoying Christ, we are transformed. In the
outer court there is no gold but brass and silver. Brass signifies
judgment and silver signifies God's redemption. Redemption
comes out of God's divine judgment. The pillars and sockets in
the outer court were of brass, but the capitals, the crowns of the
pillars, were overlaid with silver, and the hooks and the con-
necting rods were of silver (Exo. 27:11; 38:19). This indicates
that Christ's redemption comes out of the righteous judgment
of God. Christ was the One who suffered God's judgment on
the cross and out of Him comes our redemption. The sockets of

the forty-eight boards of the tabernacle were also made of silver. These forty-eight boards were made of acacia wood overlaid with gold.

All the furniture within the tabernacle was either made of gold or overlaid with gold. This signifies that the divine nature (gold) is wrought into our being by eating Christ, by feasting on Christ. By eating Him, we will be mingled with God, and this mingling transforms us. If we are going to enjoy the Lord more and more, we have to learn how to eat Him, how to feast on Him. This is a real turning point. If we know how to eat Him, how to feast on Him, we will be transformed into precious materials to be built up as the temple (1 Cor. 3:12), as the house of the Lord, and within this house we will enjoy the Lord more and more richly. As we are eating the Lord and being transformed by Him, we will enjoy the fatness of His house. We will enjoy Him to the fullest extent.

We need a vision to see that the whole Bible presents us a picture that God is the tree of life good for food to us. This is why the tree of life is at the beginning of the Bible and at the end of the Bible (Gen. 2:9; Rev. 22:2, 14). In between these two ends of the Bible are many negative stories concerning the Lord's people being distracted, frustrated, and hindered from enjoying God as the tree of life. All the positive stories in the Bible show us God's chosen people enjoying God as the tree of life in different aspects. The tree of life changed in form to a lamb because of the fall. Now we have to enjoy Him as the redeeming Lamb. After we enjoy Him in His redemptive aspect, we immediately have to enjoy Him as the nourishing, energizing Lamb. We need to learn to enjoy the Lord in such an eating way. Eating the Lord will turn us from the outer court to the holy place. By eating Him we will be transformed into precious materials to be built up with others for God's building (1 Pet. 2:5). Then there will be a house, a temple, for the Lord's rest, and in this temple we will enjoy the Lord in the fullest way. Thus, the purpose of God will be fulfilled. Finally, the house, the temple, will be enlarged to the city, which is the ultimate consummation of God's eternal intention. God's intention is realized by our eating Him. We all have to learn how to eat, how to feast, on the Lord.

The Lord Jesus became the life-giving Spirit (1 Cor. 15:45b). He is the Spirit that gives life (2 Cor. 3:6; John 6:63). We can receive this life by feeding on Him in the spirit. We have to learn how to exercise our spirit to contact the Lord. This is why the departing word of the Apostle Paul in 2 Timothy 4:22 says, "The Lord be with your spirit." The Lord Jesus is the life-giving Spirit with our spirit. We have to learn how to exercise our spirit to feed on Him, to feast on Him, to eat of Him. If we enjoy Him by the way of eating, this will turn us from outside the Lord's house to the inside, and this will transform us from pieces of clay into precious stones good for God's building.

CHAPTER SEVEN

HOW THE LAST ADAM BECOMES
THE TREE OF LIFE IN US

Scripture Reading: 1 Cor. 15:45; John 14:1-6, 10, 16-20, 23; 20:22

First Corinthians 15:45 says, "So also it is written, The first man, Adam, became a living soul; the last Adam became a life-giving Spirit." There are two important things in this verse. First, Christ, the last Adam, became a Spirit. Second, Christ was made not only a Spirit but also a life-giving, life-imparting, Spirit. He was made a Spirit for the purpose of giving life to us.

First Corinthians 15:45 does not specifically say that Christ, the Son of God, or that Jesus became a life-giving Spirit. It says that the last Adam became such a Spirit. The first Adam is the beginning of mankind; the last Adam is the ending of mankind. The last Adam means the last man. After him there are no more Adams.

HOW CHRIST BECAME A LIFE-GIVING SPIRIT

Now we have to ask how Christ became a Spirit. The explanation of how this man became a life-giving Spirit is in the Gospel of John. This Gospel begins with the Word. In the beginning was the Word, and the Word was God (John 1:1). In Him was life (v. 4). How could this life which was in Him be ours? In Him was life, but this life was not in us. The Word, which was God, became flesh; He became a man (v. 14), and this God-man was the last Adam.

In John's Gospel there are many items of Christ from chapter one to chapter fourteen. Chapter fourteen is the turning point of this Gospel. Chapter thirteen is still in the outer court. The Lord's washing of the disciples' feet in this chapter points to the washing, cleansing laver in the outer court of the tabernacle. From chapter fourteen we are turned from the outer court into the Holy Place, and from this chapter through chapter seventeen the tabernacle with the Holy Place and the Holy of Holies is built up. The Lord revealed how He would become a life-giving Spirit in John 14—16, and this way is recorded in John 18—20. This way is the way of death and resurrection. Through death and resurrection, this man became a life-giving Spirit.

In John 20 after His death and resurrection, this man came back to His disciples in the form of the Spirit and breathed into the disciples, saying, "Receive the Holy Spirit" (v. 22). The Holy Spirit is the Spirit that gives life (2 Cor. 3:6). With this Spirit, life comes into us; with this life we have light; and with this light we have all the riches of what this God-man is. All the items of Christ in the Gospel of John are the different aspects of the riches of this God-man, and all these riches are now in the life-giving Spirit. All the riches of Christ in their totality equal the life. If you have life, you enjoy the Lord as the door, the shepherd, and as so many other items. Even the footwashing in John 13 is not merely something outward. It is something inward. If you do not know how to feed on the Lord as life, you cannot enjoy life's washing. When you enjoy Him by feeding on Him as life, you will be nourished, and at the same time you will sense the washing. The nourishment washes and cleanses. When you are feeding on the Lord Jesus, eating of Him, feasting on Him, you are nourished and at the same time you are watered, enlightened, cleansed, strengthened, and comforted. The riches of this life are with the life-giving Spirit.

The book of John starts with the Word and ends with the Spirit. The Word, which is God, passed through the processes of incarnation, human living with its sufferings, crucifixion, and resurrection. In resurrection this wonderful God-man became a life-giving Spirit. All the items of what Christ is with all of His processes are condensed and included in this life-giving Spirit. You may know that Christ is the Son of God, that He is the Lamb of God who died on the cross for your sins, and that He is the Savior. But do you know Him in a living way as the life-giving Spirit?

The book of John is concluded at the end of chapter twenty with the Lord breathing Himself into the disciples as the Holy Spirit. Chapter twenty-one is the "P. S." to the Gospel of John. When we write a letter, we may have something further to say after the conclusion to make a particular point. John 21 is the "P. S." of this Gospel, proving and confirming that this life-giving Spirit is not only with but also within the disciples. Wherever they were, there the life-giving Spirit was. Even when they were fallen and backsliding, He was still there. No matter what you do, He is always with you. If you go to a movie theater, He will go with you but not happily. When the disciples backslid in John 21 by going back to the sea to take care of their living, the Lord was present with them the whole time. When Peter told the other brothers that he was going fishing, they followed him to return to their old occupation. They fished the whole night and caught nothing, but even on the land where the fish were not, the Lord could provide fish for them. Where the Lord is, our needs are taken care of. We need to learn the lesson to be one with Him. John 21 is a proof, a confirmation, that this wonderful One is now within His redeemed ones. He is with them all the time as the life-giving Spirit. John's conclusion is in chapter twenty but his "P. S." has no ending. Today we still have the "P. S." to the Gospel of John.

We have to spend some time to see the turning point of John in chapters fourteen through seventeen. John 14:1-2a says, "Let not your heart be troubled; believe in God, believe also in Me. In My Father's house are many abodes." The word "abodes" in verse 2 is the same word in Greek as "abode" in verse 23. The Lord Jesus says in this verse that He and the Father will come to the believer and make an abode with him. The word "abode" in Greek is the noun form of the verb "abide." The Lord continues in verses 2 and 3, "For I go to prepare a place for you. And if I go and prepare a place for you, I am coming again and will receive you to Myself, that where I am you also may be." The Lord said, "If I go...I am coming." This means that the Lord's going was His coming. Then He continued to say that He would receive the disciples to Himself that where He is the disciples might also be. Where is the Lord in John 14? Verse 10 says, "Do you not believe that I am in the Father, and the Father is in Me?" The Lord is in the Father and His desire was for the disciples to be where He was. He is in the Father, and they would also be in the Father. The Lord was going to do something to bring the disciples into the Father. Peter, John, James, and Andrew were not in the Father but He was. They were sinners and there was no place for them to be in the Father. Therefore, the Lord had to go (through His death and resurrection) to prepare a place for them in the Father. His desire was to bring them into the Father.

In verse 20 the Lord told the disciples, "In that day [the day of resurrection] you shall know that I am in My Father, and you in Me, and I in you." In the day of resurrection the disciples would be in the Lord and in the Father where He is. The Lord's going to the Father (v. 28) through His death and resurrection was actually His coming into the disciples (v. 18). The first step of His coming was by incarnation. The second step was His passing through death and resurrection for Him to be transfigured from the flesh into the Spirit that He might come into His disciples and dwell in them as revealed in verses 17-20. His going was really His coming.

Verses 4-6 say, "And you know where I go, and you know the way. Thomas said to Him, Lord, we do not know where You are going, and how can we know the way? Jesus said to him, I am the way, and the reality, and the life; no one comes to the Father except through Me." The way is a person and the place is also a person. Many believers interpret these verses as saying that no one can go to heaven but by Christ. But the real meaning here is that no one can go into the Father but by Christ. No one can have a real union with the Father except by Christ.

Verses 16-20 say, "And I will ask the Father, and He will give you another Comforter, that He may be with you forever; even the Spirit of reality, whom the world cannot receive, because it does not behold Him or know Him; but you know Him, because He abides with you and shall be in you. I will not leave you orphans; I am coming to you. Yet a little while and the world beholds Me no longer, but you behold Me; because I live, you shall live also. In that day you shall know that I am in My Father, and you in Me, and I in you." The very "He" who is the Spirit of reality in verse 17, becomes the very "I" who is the Lord Himself in verse 18. This means that after His resurrection, the Lord became the Spirit of reality. First Corinthians 15:45 confirms this. In dealing with the matter of resurrection, it says, "The last Adam became a life-giving Spirit." "That day" in John 14:20 should be the day of the Lord's resurrection (20:19). It should be after His resurrection that the Lord lives in His disciples and that they live by Him, as mentioned in Galatians 2:20.

Verse 23 says, "If anyone loves Me, he will keep My word, and My Father will love him, and We will come to him and make an abode with him." In John 15:4 the Lord Jesus says, "Abide in Me and I in you." In John 14 is the abode, and in chapter fifteen is the abiding. Because the abode has been prepared, the abiding is possible. The abode in 14:23 is one of the many abodes mentioned in 14:2. Eventually, it will be a mutual abode for the Triune God to abide in the believers and for the believers to abide in Him.

The book of John reveals to us that we have sin (16:8-9), and in John 12:31 the ruler of this world, the king of this age, the enemy of God, Satan the Devil, is mentioned. We human beings are sinful and are under the hand of this usurping one, Satan. With the problem of sin and of Satan how could we have a union with God the Father? How could we get into the Father, and how could the Father get into us? The Lord Jesus came to bring us into the Father and to bring the Father into us. He came that we might have life and that we might have it abundantly (John 10:10). But how could this be accomplished since we are sinful and are under the hand of Satan? First, the Lamb had to be slain, had to die, for our sins (1:29). The Lamb had to be put on the cross to shed His blood so that our sins could be dealt with. Also, when He was lifted up on the cross, Satan was judged and cast out (12:31-32). By His death He solved the problem of sin and the problem of Satan, thus preparing the way that we might get into the Father to have a place in the Father. He went to prepare a place for us in the Father by shedding His blood to redeem us from our sins and to wash away all our sins, and by destroying His enemy Satan, thus releasing us from Satan's usurping hand. The Lord was not going to heaven to prepare a heavenly mansion for us in order that we might go there one day after we die. This thought does not correspond with the entire Gospel of John. The Lord came that He might bring God into man and that He might bring man into God. But we have the problems of sin, Satan, and the world. These negative things separated us from God and hindered God from coming into us. All these problems were solved and dealt with by the Lord's all-inclusive death. By His crucifixion, sins, the world, and Satan have been done away with. By His death He has prepared the way, and He has even prepared a place that where He is we also may be. He is in the Father and through His death and resurrection we can also be in the Father. He was going to prepare a place for us in the Father.

On the positive side, the Lord came that He might impart Himself into us as life. For this He went to the cross as a grain of wheat (John 12:24). A grain of wheat imparts its life into other grains by death and resurrection. When a grain of wheat falls into the earth and dies, it grows up and the life within it is imparted into many grains. Through death and resurrection the life within the one grain becomes the life of many grains. It is in this way that the Lord imparted Himself into us. By having Him within us, we are one with Him. He is in the Father, and we also are in the Father by His death and resurrection. By His all-inclusive death and His wonderful resurrection, He has brought Himself into us and He has brought us into Himself and into the Father. This is why He says, "In that day you shall know that I am in My Father, and you in Me, and I in you." Through His death and resurrection He became our abode and we became His abodes. We are in Him, so He is our abode; and He is in us, so we are His abodes. By His death and resurrection many abodes were prepared. All these abodes added together equal the Father's house.

The term "the Father's house" is used in the Gospel of John

in 2:16 and 14:2. In chapter two the Father's house is the temple, and in chapter 14 it is the same. To say that the Father's house is heaven is not according to the biblical revelation. The Father's house is the building, the temple, which is the total of all the abodes, the total of all the regenerated people. In the Father's house there are many abodes. The Father's house is actually a mutual abode, a mingling of the Triune God with His chosen, redeemed, and regenerated people. To the Father, the Son, and the Spirit, we are the abodes, and to us They are the abode. This is the mutual abode revealed in the Gospel of John. We have been brought into the Triune God and the Triune God has been wrought into us in the way of mingling. The Lord Jesus was going in order to die and resurrect that He might bring us into the Father and that He might bring the Father into us, thus accomplishing the universal mingling of the Triune God with humanity. This mingling is the Father's house.

The Lord Jesus brought the Father into us by the Spirit and in the Spirit. John 14—16 shows us that through death and resurrection the last man, the last Adam, became a life-giving Spirit. Thus, on the evening of His resurrection, He came to the disciples not in the form of the flesh but in the form of the Spirit. He is the Spirit in resurrection.

THE SPIRIT BEING AN ALL-INCLUSIVE DOSE

This Spirit is an all-inclusive dose. With this Spirit, there is redemption, the released life, and the overcoming resurrection of Christ. Within this all-inclusive dose is the cleansing element, which cleanses away all our sins, cleanses away the world, and cleanses away even Satan. To deal with the negative side, the cleansing, redeeming element is within the Spirit. On the positive side, the life-imparting element, the nourishing element, the supplying element, is within this Spirit. Whenever someone opens himself to the Lord Jesus to receive Him as his Savior, this Spirit immediately comes into him with the redeeming power and with the imparting power, redeeming him from all the negative things and imparting into him all the positive things.

GRAFTED INTO CHRIST TO ENJOY CHRIST

By this Spirit we are delivered from all the negative things, and in this Spirit we have been grafted into Christ, becoming the branches of the vine tree revealed in John 15. Christ Himself is the vine tree, and we believers are the many branches of this tree. We have been grafted into Christ by this all-inclusive Spirit. When we believed into Jesus as the Savior, this all-inclusive Spirit came into us, delivering us from all the negative things on the negative side, and grafting us into Christ so that we might become a branch of Christ on the positive side.

This life-giving Spirit, who is Christ Himself, who is the Word that was God, who is the Son of God, and who is the reality of the Triune God, is within us. We have to learn not only to feed on Him, to eat of Him, but also to abide in Him. John 1:12-13 tells us that we have to receive Him and that to believe in Him is to receive Him. The book of John also tells us that we have to drink of Him (4:14; 7:37) and that we have to eat Him (John 6:57). Furthermore, John tells us that we have to abide in Him (15:4). The order in John is to receive Him, to drink of Him, to eat Him, and to abide in Him. In order to abide in Him we first have to receive Him. Then we have to learn how to drink of Him and feed on Him. By drinking of Him and feeding on Him, we can abide in Him.

We all have to realize the reality of the tree of life. God's intention is to present Himself to us as the tree of life. We not only eat of this tree, but we also are abiding in this tree. Not only do we take something of the tree into us, but we also have become a part of the tree. By drinking of the Lord and by feeding on Him we become a part of Him; we become the branches of the tree. For the branches to absorb the life juice of the tree is the real drinking. The branches are drinking of the tree and eating of the tree by absorbing the life juice of the tree. The branches absorb all that the tree is and has and also abide in the tree, have their existence in the tree. Without the tree, the branches can do nothing and they cannot even live or exist. It is in the tree that they have their existence.

This tree in which we have our existence is the Triune God. The Word that was God became flesh, died, and resurrected, being transfigured into a life-giving Spirit. Today the processed Triune God is the life-giving Spirit. What a wonderful fact that today there is such a life-giving Spirit! The Triune God has passed through many processes to become an all-inclusive dose so available to each one of us. This universal, eternal life-giving Spirit, who is Christ the Lord, is waiting for man to receive Him. As many as receive Him, He gives them the authority to become the sons of God. Now we need to learn how to drink of Him, how to feed on Him, and then we have to abide in Him. We have to realize that we are His branches. We have to feed on Him in the way of absorbing all that He is to us. If we would abide in Him, absorbing all that He is, we will experience the killing element within Him. In the all-inclusive dose, there is the germ-killing element, dealing with our flesh, our self, Satan, and the world.

The more you try to put yourself to death by reckoning yourself to be dead, the more you will be alive. Brother Watchman Nee once told us that a person can commit suicide in many ways, but no one can commit suicide by means of crucifixion. To be crucified there is the need of others to put you on the cross. You cannot nail yourself to the cross. Forget about putting yourself to death. Just feed on Him and abide in Him. The more you absorb the life juice of Christ as the tree of life, the more you will sense the killing element within you.

The Triune God is the tree of life to us and we can share of this tree of life because of His incarnation plus His death and resurrection. By His incarnation He brought God into man, and by His death and resurrection He has brought man into God. Also, by His death and resurrection, He became a Spirit; He was transfigured from the flesh into the Spirit, a life-giving Spirit. This life-giving Spirit brings God into us and brings us into God. He grafts us into Christ, the universal tree, to make us branches of this tree. Now we need to enjoy all that He is. Through our abiding and our enjoying Him, the church will come into existence as the real expression of the Triune God. Out of our enjoyment and experience of the tree of life, God's eternal purpose will be fulfilled. How important it is that we know this tree of life and that we experience this tree of life in such a living way!

CHAPTER EIGHT

HOW THE BODY, THE ARMY, AND THE DWELLING PLACE OF GOD CAME INTO BEING

Scripture Reading: Rev. 2:7, 17; 3:20; Ezek. 1:1, 27; 37:1-12, 14, 26-28; 47:1-12; 48:30-35

THE IMPORTANCE OF EATING

In three of the last seven epistles written by the Lord to the churches in the book of Revelation, He talks about the matter of eating as a reward to the overcomers. The eating of the tree of life is mentioned first and then the eating of the manna. In the first epistle He talks about eating the tree of life (2:7), which was mentioned at the very beginning of the divine revelation in Genesis 2. In the third epistle the Lord talks about eating the hidden manna (2:17). Manna was first revealed in Exodus 16. In the last epistle the Lord concludes by saying that He stands at the door and knocks. Whoever is willing to open the door to let the Lord come in, the Lord will dine with that person (3:20). These seven epistles open and close with the matter of eating.

We have seen clearly from the Scriptures that eating transforms us. This can be realized even with our physical eating of food. If a person does not eat for three days, he will look weak and pale. But once he eats a few good meals, his appearance will be transformed. He will be shining instead of pale and strong instead of weak. We are transformed by eating. If you eat beef day after day, you will begin to have the odor of beef. You will have the odor of a cow because you have eaten so much cow. Eating transforms.

Previously, we have seen that eating is the turning point from the outer court of the tabernacle into the Holy Place. In the outer court of the tabernacle at the altar are all the offerings. We can enjoy Christ's redemption through these offerings. After enjoying the redemptive aspect of the offerings, the priests had to eat most of the offerings. The eating started with the offerings in the outer court.

By eating the offerings the priests are turned into the tabernacle. In the Holy Place of the tabernacle is the showbread table. The priests were to eat the showbread in the Holy Place (Lev. 24:5-9). According to the mentioning of the items within the tabernacle, the showbread table was the first item on the north, and on the south was the lampstand (Exo. 26:35). The life we enjoy in the showbread issues in the light of the lampstand. The eating of the bread is the enjoyment of life and this life is the light of men (John 1:4), the light of life (8:12). Next in the tabernacle is the incense altar. The sweetness of Christ follows the enlightening.

In the outer court the first item is redemption, that is, justification by faith through the blood. Based upon this justification through redemption, you are entitled to enjoy the eating of all the offerings which are the different aspects of Christ. Through Christ's redemption, you are entitled and have the ground to enjoy Christ as your portion. You have to eat of Him. Thus, eating is the last item in the outer court, but the first item in the Holy Place. At the showbread table, the priest continues to eat.

In the Holy of Holies, the first item within the ark is the hidden manna. Also within the ark are the enlightening law, matching the lampstand, and the sprouting, budding rod of Aaron, signifying our experience of Christ in His resurrection as our acceptance by God and matching the sweetness of the incense (Heb. 9:3-4). Either in the Holy Place or in the Holy of Holies, eating is the main item in our pursuit of the Lord.

Eating transforms us into precious material for God's building. With the tabernacle are the wooden boards overlaid with gold based upon the silver sockets (Exo. 26:15-25, 29-30). This means that by eating Christ, based upon His redemption signified by the silver sockets, we will be transformed, overlaid with the divine nature, which is the gold. By eating Christ based upon His redemption, something divine will be wrought into us and upon us. Eventually there is a tabernacle built up with wood and gold mingled together. This mingling is accomplished by eating. Wood signifies us, and gold signifies God. How could God become a part of us? How could we be in the nature of God? How could the nature of God overlay us? By our eating Him.

Eating involves three things. First, eating means to take something into you. Second, without eating we cannot exist. I may have life, but I need to eat to maintain this life. Third, whatever I take in is what I live by, and what I take in will be digested by me and become my very constituent, my very element. What I eat becomes a part of me. In John 6 the Lord tells us that He is the bread of life (v. 35) and that the one who eats Him will live because of Him (v. 57).

The entire Bible reveals to us one central thing—God's intention is to work Himself into us. First Corinthians 6:17 says, "He who is joined to the Lord is one spirit." God's intention is to make Himself one with us. This is something so marvelous. No human mind could ever imagine that such a thing could happen in the universe, that is, that the Creator and almighty God intends to make Himself one with us. There is only one way that God could be one with us. God can work Himself into us to be one with us by the way of eating. God presented Himself to man as the tree of life immediately after man's creation. God as the tree of life is for eating. Not only in Genesis 2 but also in Revelation 2 we are told to eat of the tree of life.

The tree of life is the Triune God—the Father embodied in the Son and the Son realized as the Spirit. The tree of life is the very Triune God embodied and realized. The Father is the very source, and all the fullness of this source dwells in the Son. The Son is the embodiment of the source, and the Son is realized as the Spirit. The Spirit comes into us with all the fullness of the source that we may enjoy Him and take Him as food. This is the central thought of the entire Scripture. The Scripture opens with the tree of life and closes with the tree of life. What we take into us is what we live by. What we take into us is digested by us and becomes our very constituent, our very element. What has been taken into us will become one with us and will become us. We need to learn to feed on the Triune God and to enjoy Him all day long. Out of this eating comes the tabernacle.

After the tabernacle was the temple, which also was the issue of eating. The six books in the Old Testament from 1 Samuel to 2 Chronicles give us a full record of the building of the temple. If you read these books carefully, you will see that the temple was a product of the enjoyment of all the produce of the good land of Canaan. The good land of Canaan typifies the all-inclusive, resurrected, and ascended Christ. The middle portion of the good land was offered to God in Ezekiel as a heave offering (48:8-12), typifying Christ resurrected and lifted up, ascended to the heavens. The land of Canaan was an elevated land, high above sea level, signifying the resurrected and ascended Christ. God has brought us into this land and has put us into Christ. Now we are living in this land. Now we are living in Christ, walking in Christ, and even laboring on Christ. Day by day we labor on this good land, on Christ. Then we have the produce of Christ not only to enjoy privately but also to enjoy publicly and corporately with God by offering this surplus of the produce of the good land to God. It was through this that the temple was built, which is a type of the church. The temple was the issue of the enjoyment of all the produce of the good land, typifying how the church comes into existence by our enjoyment of Christ.

Christ is the elevated land. He is typified by the land resurrected from the death waters on the third day in Genesis 1 (vv. 9, 13). On the third day the land came out of the water; this land is the resurrected Christ. We live in Him, walk in Him, labor on Him, and then we enjoy Him. We enjoy all the riches of life, the different aspects of life. Many different aspects of life came out of this elevated land in Genesis 1, showing that all the riches of life come out of the resurrected and ascended Christ. We just need to labor on Him and enjoy Him. The result, the issue, of this enjoyment of Christ is the building up of the church.

The Pharisees and the scribes learned the objective teachings of the Old Testament, but they were the ones who plotted to put the Lord on the cross. The Lord told the Jewish religionists that they searched the Scriptures, but they were not willing to come to Him that they might have life (John 5:39-40). To search the Bible for knowledge is one thing, but to come to the Lord to contact Him for life is another thing. The priests and the scribes had the knowledge concerning the birth of Christ, but they did not have the heart to seek after Christ as did the Magi from the east (Matt. 2:1-12). The learned Gentiles, the Magi, did not know the Scriptures concerning where Christ would be born, but they went to the newborn King.

The Christian life is not a matter merely of knowledge, but a matter of eating. Do not merely consider the church meetings to be like a school. You have to take the church meetings as a restaurant. Do not come to the meetings just to learn, but come to eat, to feed on the Lord. People do not go to a restaurant just to learn how to read the menu. Whenever we go to the restaurant, we do not go for the menu. We just care for one thing—eating. Learn to eat the Lord. Knowledge puffs up, but love in life builds up (1 Cor. 8:1). We have to learn how to enjoy the Lord. Strictly speaking, the Bible is not merely for us to learn but for us to eat. Man lives not only by bread but also by every word that proceeds out from the mouth of God (Matt. 4:4). The word from the mouth of God is our food, not merely knowledge or teachings.

All the Bible's teachings are for Christ. The menu's purpose is for eating. You should not take the menu as the eating itself. We have to be brought back from the distracting knowledge and the distracting teachings to this one thing—the enjoyment of the living Lord as the life-giving Spirit. Learn to deal with Him and to be dealt with by Him. Learn to contact Him. Learn to dwell upon Him. Learn to labor on Him. Then God's purpose will be fulfilled. Then the desire of God will be attained. God's desire for the temple, the dwelling place, the universal building for God to rest in, can be realized by our eating of the Lord, by having the Lord mingle Himself with us. There is only one way for the Lord to get into us and for Him to mingle Himself with us and that is by our eating Him.

We have to keep the principle of the first mentioning in the Bible. After the creation of man, the first thing mentioned about the relationship between man and God is man's eating. The first picture in the Bible shows us that God presented Himself to man in the form of food and that man had to learn how to eat of Him, how to take Him in, how to live by Him, and how to digest Him in order to have Him be man's very constituent. By this matter of eating, God can attain His desire and fulfill His purpose.

THE LORD AS THE JUDGING FIRE, THE BREATHING AIR, AND THE FLOWING WATER

Also in the Old Testament there is a prophecy about the temple to come in the book of Ezekiel. In the book of Ezekiel there are three great chapters—chapter one, chapter thirty-seven, and chapter forty-seven. In chapter one there is fire (vv. 4, 27). In chapter thirty-seven there is air or wind, breath, Spirit (vv. 9, 14). And in chapter forty-seven there is water (vv. 1-12). These are the three great chapters of Ezekiel and the contents of this book depend on these three things: fire, air, and water, which are the Lord God Himself. Our God is a consuming fire, our God is the air, and our God is the water.

The first part of Ezekiel reveals to us how God is the fire to judge by burning. God is a burning fire to burn away all things which do not correspond with His divine nature. After this burning, God came in to breathe. After the burning is the breathing. After the fire is the air. The air, the breath, is the divine Spirit. The air came into the dead and dry bones, which were under the judgment of the fire, to quicken them, to make them alive, and to give them all that they need in order to constitute them into a body. The breath (Heb. *ruach*) put into these dead and dry bones is the very Spirit of God Himself (Ezek. 37:5, 6, 14). The body comes from the air, from the breath, from the life-giving Spirit.

After the dead bones were made alive, they became three things: the body (Ezek. 37:7-8), the army (v. 10), and the dwelling place (vv. 26-28). The body lives for God, the army fights for God, and the dwelling place is for God to rest in. All the dead bones were constituted into a living body, and this living body became a fighting army. Eventually, this fighting army became the very resting place of God. When we can live with God and fight for God, we can be the resting place to God. The temple, the house of God, comes from the enjoyment of the Lord as life, as the life-giving Spirit. When we enjoy the Lord as the breathing element, we will become alive, we will grow, and we will be built up. Originally we may have been pieces of bone, but now we can be built up as a body and formed as an army to become a dwelling place for God to rest in. This building, this temple, this house of God, comes out of the very enjoyment of God as our life.

Many Christians are indifferent to the things of the Lord and are worldly and even sinful, backsliding far away from the Lord. There are, however, some seeking ones among the Lord's children who have been revived by the Lord and to a certain extent experience the Lord. But many of them have been distracted to pay their full attention to the study of the Word merely for the sake of gaining more knowledge. Teachings and knowledge could not make the dry bones in Ezekiel 37 alive. Do the dry bones need the teachings or the letter of the Word? No! They need the air; they need the breathing; they need the breath. And who is the air? God is the air; He is the *ruach,* the *pneuma.* What we need is this life-giving God, this life-giving Spirit.

Fire judges, consumes, and burns; air quickens, generates, energizes, strengthens, enriches, and builds. After the building was set up in Ezekiel, the water flowed out from the building to water others. Before the flowing out of the water in Ezekiel 47, there is a desert everywhere with only death and dryness. But by the flow of this living water out of the house every part will be watered (vv. 8-9). Death is swallowed up and life is ministered to all these dead, dry places. The book of Ezekiel reveals judgment by fire, quickening, life-giving, by air, and ministering by water. These three steps are still with us today in principle. We first have to be judged, to be burned by the Lord as fire. Then the Lord will be as the air to breathe upon us. By this breathing we will be quickened, regenerated, and we will grow up and be built up. After the building is set up, the living water will flow out to water

us. The real content of the book of Ezekiel is the Lord as the
judging fire, burning and consuming, the Lord as the breathing air, regenerating, strengthening, and building up, and the
Lord as the flowing water, ministering Himself to the dry
places. All this can only be possible by our eating of the Lord.

EATING THE LORD TO BE MINGLED WITH HIM
FOR THE BUILDING OF THE CHURCH

In the last chapter of Ezekiel there is a city foursquare with
three gates on every side (48:30-35). Three times four equals
twelve. Three refers to the Triune God and four refers to the
creatures such as the four living creatures. In God's building
there is the number three. The first building of God was the ark
of Noah. The ark of Noah had three stories, signifying God the
Father, God the Son, and God the Spirit. With God's building
there is always the number three because the Triune God is
there. Three plus four means that God is added to man. At the
beginning of Revelation are the seven churches; seven is three
plus four. But the consummate number in the New Jerusalem
is twelve, signifying God multiplying Himself with man, God
mingling Himself with man. Addition becomes multiplication.
Thus, the outcome of the book of Ezekiel is the number twelve,
the mingling of the Triune God with the created man. At the
end of Revelation there is the same thing—a city foursquare
with three gates on every side, signifying the Triune God mingled with man. This mingling can only be realized by our
eating. Many American eggs have been mingled with some of us
by our eating of these eggs. We have to learn to eat the Lord to
be mingled with Him.

This is why the Lord Jesus, in His last seven epistles to
the churches in Revelation, told us clearly that He will give
the one who overcomes to eat of the tree of life, which is the
Triune God Himself for our enjoyment. He also promises to
give the overcomer to eat of the hidden manna. When the
church is so worldly and even married with the world like
the church in Pergamos, the Lord will give the hidden
manna, the private manna, which is the Lord Himself, to the
overcomers. Finally, in these seven epistles, the Lord Jesus
told us that if we have an ear to hear His voice and open the

door, He will come in not to teach us but to dine with us, to feast with us, so that we can enjoy Him and He can enjoy us.

The church life is the enjoyment of the tree of life, the hidden manna, and the divine feast. We feast with the Lord and let the Lord feast with us. From this eating, from this mingling, the building up of the house of God will be realized. Here is the way of the church life. The church life is not something produced by organizing power, by teaching, or even by gifts, but something produced by eating the Lord as the tree of life, as the hidden manna, and as the feast.

CHAPTER NINE

CHRIST OPENS THE WAY
TO THE TREE OF LIFE

Scripture Reading: Gen. 3:22-24; Heb. 4:12, 14-16; 10:19-20

THE REQUIREMENTS OF GOD'S GLORY,
GOD'S RIGHTEOUSNESS, AND GOD'S HOLINESS
FULFILLED BY THE DEATH OF CHRIST

Genesis 3:22-24 says, "And the Lord God said, Behold, the man is become as one of us, to know good and evil: and now, lest he put forth his hand, and take also of the tree of life, and eat, and live forever: therefore the Lord God sent him forth from the garden of Eden, to till the ground from whence he was taken. So he drove out the man: and he placed at the east of the garden of Eden cherubim, and a flaming sword which turned every way, to keep the way of the tree of life." Cherubim signify the glory of God (Heb. 9:5). The requirement of the glory of God closes the way to the tree of life from fallen man. The sword signifies judgment by God's righteousness. We have to fulfill God's righteousness; otherwise, we are under the judgment of God. Fire signifies God's holiness. The requirements of God's glory, God's righteousness, and God's holiness kept fallen man from the tree of life. Until these requirements could be fully met, the way to the tree of life could never be open to fallen man.

Hebrews 4:14-16 says, "Having therefore a great High Priest who has passed through the heavens, Jesus, the Son of God, let us hold fast the confession. For we do not have a high priest who is not able to sympathize with our weaknesses, but One who has been tried in all respects like us, yet without sin. Let us therefore come forward with boldness to the throne of grace, that we may receive mercy and may find grace for timely help." In these three verses, there is Christ as the High Priest ascended to the heavens. Second, this ascended Christ can sympathize with our weaknesses. Although He is in the heavens and we are on this earth, He can be touched by the feeling of our infirmities. Third, in verse 16 we are charged to come to the throne of grace. Verse 14 tells us that Christ, who is on the throne of grace, is in the heavens. How then can we come to the throne of grace in the heavens? Before we solve this problem, let us read verses 12 and 13 of chapter four: "For the word of God is living and operative and sharper than any two-edged sword, and piercing even to the dividing of soul and spirit, both of joints and marrow, and able to discern the thoughts and intents of the heart. And there is no creature that is not manifest before Him, but all things are naked and laid bare to the eyes of Him to whom we are accountable." Hebrews 10:19-20 says, "Having therefore, brothers, boldness for entering the Holy of Holies by the blood of Jesus, by a new and living way, which He dedicated for us through the veil, that is, His flesh." In these verses we are told that we have the boldness to enter the Holy of Holies. The throne of grace is equivalent to the mercy seat in the Holy of Holies (Exo. 25:17, 21). Thus, to come to the throne of grace means to come into the Holy of Holies. We enter into the Holy of Holies by the blood of Jesus, by a new and living way.

We have seen that the tree of life is nothing less than God Himself in His Trinity presented to us. But due to the fall of the human race, man became sinful and the way to the tree of life was closed. Man had fallen short of the glory of God (Rom. 3:23). Man was also under the condemnation of God's righteousness, and man was against God's holiness. God's desire was still that man would enjoy Him as the tree of life, but His glory, His righteousness, and His holiness kept fallen man away from the tree of life. No fallen man can get through these three items—the cherubim, the slaying sword, and the flaming fire. If man is going to eat the tree of life, he has to fulfill the requirements of God's glory, God's righteousness, and God's holiness.

On the one hand, man's fallen condition, man's sin, has to be solved, has to be taken away. On the other hand, all the requirements of God's glory, God's righteousness, and God's holiness have to be fulfilled. Otherwise, there is no way for human beings to eat the tree of life. Where is the tree of life? The tree of life is in the Holy of Holies. How could a sinful person get through the outer court, enter into the Holy Place, and pass through the inner veil into the Holy of Holies to eat the tree of life? On the altar in the outer court, the sacrifices dealt with the fallen condition and the sins of man. The altar typifies the cross of Christ. On the cross, not only was sin dealt with, but also the veil was rent (Heb. 10:20). This is the second veil (9:3) within the tabernacle, which typifies the flesh of Christ. When Christ's flesh was crucified, this veil was rent (Matt. 27:51), thus opening the way for us who were excluded from God, signified by the tree of life (Gen. 3:22-24), to enter into the Holy of Holies to contact Him and take Him as the tree of life for our enjoyment. Christ, the eternal all-inclusive sacrifice, died on the cross, on the altar. He fulfilled all the requirements of God's righteousness, God's holiness, and God's glory. By His death, Christ opened the way for us to eat God as the tree of life. This is why Christ told us in John 14 that He had to go to prepare a place for us.

The Gospel of John tells us that the Word who was God became flesh (1:14), and this is the Christ, the Messiah (v. 41), the One who is the life (14:6), the light (8:12), the food (6:35), the drink (7:37-38), the air (20:22), the shepherd (10:11), the door (10:1), and so many other items. How could Christ be so many things to us? We have sin within, and we commit sins without. If Christ is going to impart Himself to us as so many things, He has to solve the problem of sin and sins. God's glory, righteousness, and holiness would not allow Him to impart Himself to such sinful persons. Therefore, Christ had to fulfill the requirements of God's glory, righteousness, and holiness through His death on the cross.

HOW THE GOD-MAN WAS MADE AVAILABLE TO US

Now we need to see how this God-man could be made available to us. As an illustration, let us use the example of a family partaking of a watermelon. The parents would not let their children eat with dirty hands. The children would have to first wash their hands before they ate the watermelon.

Then the melon has to be cut into pieces. When the slices are eaten by the children, they become juice for easy digestion. On the one hand, the children are cleansed; on the other hand, juice is available for them to digest. The Triune God has been processed in a similar fashion. In order for the watermelon to get into the children the sequence is first watermelon, then slices, and finally juice. The Father is illustrated by the whole melon; the Son by the slices; and finally, the Spirit by the juice. The Father is not only the Father, but is also the Son. And the Son is not only the Son, but is also the Spirit. In other words, this melon is also the slices to eat and the juice within us. The melon disappears after it is eaten. Originally, the melon was on the table, but after being eaten, the melon is in the whole family. The Father is in the Son, and the Son is the Spirit, who is just like the juice. Actually, the Spirit is more available than the juice because the Spirit is air (Gk. *pneuma* and Heb. *ruach*). Both *pneuma* and *ruach* can be translated into four English words—air, breath, wind, and spirit. Christ, the God-man, in resurrection became a life-giving Spirit. This big melon became the refreshing juice.

LEARNING TO EXERCISE OUR SPIRIT
TO CONTACT AND ENJOY CHRIST

By His death Christ did away with all the negative things such as our sinful nature and our sins. He has cleansed us with His precious blood and in His resurrection He became a life-giving Spirit. He was transfigured into a life-giving Spirit. Now we are prepared and He is available. All that is needed is for us to enjoy Him. After the children's hands have been washed, cleansed, and the juice is available, it would be stupid for the children to listen to the watermelon or to look at the watermelon and not eat it. Many of us have been like this toward the Lord. Throughout our Christian life, we have been listening, learning, seeing, reading, and studying, but we have not been eating. We have been starving, yet we did not feel hungry. If we are in desperate need of food and do not feel hungry, this means that we are sick. The Lord rebuked the church in Laodicea because they said that they were rich, when they were really poor (Rev. 3:17). They were poor, yet they did not have the feeling or the sense that they were poor. They thought that they were rich. They thought that they knew everything. They had all the doctrines, but they did not have the goal. They did not have the Lord Himself dining with them. May the Lord be merciful to us and deliver us from the doctrines and from the teachings that distract us from the enjoyment of Christ.

We all have to learn to eat and drink the Lord by exercising the proper organ to take Him in. The proper organ is our spirit. Our wonderful Lord, the tree of life, the Word become flesh, the God-man, died to pave the way and to prepare the place. Through His death, He has done away with all the negative things and we are cleansed. In His resurrection He has also become a life-giving Spirit. If we are going to contact this Spirit, we have to exercise our spirit. "God is Spirit; and those who worship Him must worship in spirit..." (John 4:24). We should not merely exercise our mind to understand, to learn, and to study, but we should exercise our spirit to contact Him, to drink Him, and to eat Him. By His blood, our conscience has been purged, so our spirit is cleansed and free from any kind of condemnation. We have the peace to contact Him. The more we open ourselves to the Lord from our spirit, the more we have the peace and the sense that He is one with us. We can contact Him as the life-giving Spirit within us and enjoy the Lord.

This is why Hebrews 4:12 tells us that the spirit must be divided from the soul. The soul is the real problem. The background of the book of Hebrews is related to the Judaizers distracting people from the enjoyment of Christ. They may have told a Hebrew believer, "We are the descendants of our forefathers who received the law from our God. We have to believe in Jesus, yet we shouldn't give up the law." This doctrinal argument would have confused the Hebrew believers. Paul wrote Hebrews to tell these Christians that we have to deal with the living Christ and to enjoy this living Christ, not to deal with a religion. We do not need a religion, but we need a living Person, who is Christ as the tree of life. If we are going to deal with a religion, we need the soul, the mind. But if we are going to deal with a living Person, who is Christ, the life-giving Spirit, we have to learn how to exercise our spirit. Our spirit has to be divided from our disturbing and deceived soul. We have to discern our spirit from this deceived and disturbing soul. We have to learn to exercise our spirit to contact and enjoy Christ, the life-giving Spirit.

On the one hand, Christ is in the heavens. On the other hand, He is in our spirit. With the resurrected and ascended Christ there is no problem of space or time. He is the same yesterday, today, and forever (Heb. 13:8). He is like the air. With the air there is no problem of space or time. As the air, Christ is everywhere. He is heavenly, not earthly, and He is spiritual, not fleshly. We must learn how to exercise our spirit to contact this heavenly and spiritual Christ, who is the life-giving Spirit. With us there is the problem of yesterday, today, and tomorrow. We may tell others not to come to see us after midnight. But the Lord never would tell us not to contact Him after midnight. He is available any time.

Air is different from food. We take food at certain times, but we breathe the air at all times, even when we are sleeping. With the air there is no problem of time or space. A person may be so busy that he even forgets to eat, but he will never be too busy to forget to breathe. Whenever we turn to the Lord and wherever we are, He is there as the divine air, the divine *pneuma*. Where He is, there is the Holy of Holies. Where He is, there is the throne of grace. Our contacting Him depends only on one thing—the exercise of our spirit. We have to touch, to sense, to heed His indwelling presence. If we use the wrong organ, His presence will be hidden from us. If we try to look at a fragrance in the air, we are using the wrong organ. If we exercise our sense of smell, we will immediately sense and enjoy the fragrance.

All the obstacles, hindrances, and negative things, such as the world, Satan the devil, the demons, darkness, sin, sins, and the flesh have been done away with, and all the requirements of God's glory, God's righteousness, and God's holiness have been fully met. There is no problem for us to contact God. Furthermore, God has gone through a process so that He could be available to us. The melon has been made into juice.

The Triune God became a man, and this God-man, Jesus, became a life-giving Spirit. Everything is prepared, and He is so available, just like the air. He is waiting for us to do one thing—to exercise our spirit. When we exercise our spirit to contact the Lord, we sense that we are in the Holy of Holies and that we are touching the throne of grace. We can obtain the needed mercy and find grace flowing within us as the living water to be our timely help. This is the way to enjoy the tree of life today. I believe the Lord will recover the experience of the tree of life among His children.

By His all-inclusive death and His wonderful resurrection, He has paved the way and has prepared the place. It is now so easy for us to get into the Father and so easy for the Father to be brought into us. Everything is done, all has been prepared, and Christ has become a life-giving Spirit. The life-giving Spirit is the ultimate expression of the Triune God. He was the Creator, the almighty God, and as the Word He became flesh. He is the God-man who passed through death and resurrection to become a life-giving Spirit. This life-giving Spirit is the Creator, the almighty God, the Father, the Son, and the Spirit. Included in this life-giving Spirit are Christ's incarnation, human living, crucifixion, resurrection, and ascension. God's righteousness, holiness, and glory and the fulfillment of all the requirements are also included in the life-giving Spirit. He is so available. All we need to do is receive this Spirit by calling on the name of the Lord (1 Cor. 12:3; Acts 2:17a, 21). Then we will enjoy Him within.

The book of Hebrews tells us that we have to be delivered from religion into this living Person. We have to give up religion to take this living One. It needs sixty-six books of the Bible to define who this living One is. This marvelous and wonderful living One is as available as the air. All of our troubles and problems have been solved by His all-inclusive death. Our conscience, the main part of our spirit, has been fully purged and thoroughly cleansed. We should have the full peace, the full confidence, the full boldness, and the full assurance to come to contact Him. We can come into the Holiest Place and touch the throne of grace to enjoy Him as mercy and as grace, as the flowing water and as the enjoyable life.

As the life-giving Spirit, He is like the refreshing air. Wherever we are and whenever we turn to Him, He is there. The only thing we need to realize is that we have to exercise our spirit to contact Him. When we exercise our spirit to contact Him, we are in the Holy of Holies touching the throne of grace and enjoying the source of grace, the life-giving Spirit. This is the enjoyment of the tree of life, which will transform us, equip us, strengthen us, clothe us, and even adorn us with Christ. Out of this enjoyment we all will be built up together as the building, the resting place, of God.

At the end of the Bible there is a universal building (Rev. 21:2). The throne is the center of this building, and out of this throne flows a river of living water (22:1). The tree of life grows in the flow of the water to supply all of God's redeemed (v. 2). This must not be a doctrine to us but must be something experienced by us day by day and hour by hour. The Lord needs a group of people to enjoy Him, to partake of Him, and to experience Him in such a living way that they may come together to be His living expression. With them there will be God's image to express the Triune God, God's authority to represent the ruling Lord, and God's life within to fulfill all the requirements. All of this depends on one thing—the enjoyment of the Triune God as the tree of life. We need to ask the Lord to make the fellowship in this chapter a heavenly vision to us and beseech Him to bring us into the reality of this vision.

CHAPTER TEN

GOD'S PURPOSE FULFILLED
BY THE GROWTH
OF THE TREE OF LIFE WITHIN US

Scripture Reading: Matt. 13:3, 8; John 3:5; Luke 17:21; Gal.
5:22; Psa. 34:8; 1 Pet. 2:2-3; 3:7; 2 Pet. 1:3-4; Acts 5:20; Rom.
5:10, 21

FULFILLING THE REQUIREMENTS OF GOD'S GLORY,
GOD'S HOLINESS, AND GOD'S RIGHTEOUSNESS
TO ENJOY THE TRIUNE GOD

God's intention is to work Himself into us as our life in the
form of food by our eating of Him. But man became fallen.
Due to the fall of man, man became involved with Satan, with
the evil force of darkness. All the negative things in this universe are related to man due to his fall. Before man was
created, Satan, the darkness of Satan, and the evil kingdom
of Satan were there already, but man had nothing to do with
these negative things. By the fall, Satan brought all these
negative things to man, which are against God's glory, God's
holiness, and God's righteousness. God's glory, holiness, and
righteousness would not allow fallen man to touch God. However, the all-inclusive death of Christ dealt with and did away
with all these negative things. Furthermore, through His
death and in His resurrection Christ became a life-giving
Spirit. He has made Himself available for us to enjoy. The
Triune God embodied in Christ who is realized as the life-
giving Spirit is the central outcome of all the works which
Christ has accomplished.

The tabernacle of the Old Testament shows us that the
Triune God is for our enjoyment. There are three parts to

the tabernacle—the outer court, the Holy Place, and the Holy of Holies. In the outer court is the righteousness of God; in the Holy Place is the holiness of God; and in the Holy of Holies is the glory of God. If you are going to pass the outer court, you have to fulfill the requirements of God's righteousness; if you are going to get into the Holy Place, you have to fulfill the requirements of God's holiness; and if you are going to get into the Holy of Holies, you need to fulfill the requirements of God's glory. In the Holy of Holies is God Himself. The ark of testimony is the very embodiment of God and inside the ark is the hidden manna, which signifies that God is our enjoyment. At the conclusion of the divine revelation, the New Jerusalem is called the tabernacle of God (Rev. 21:2-3). This tabernacle is a total, ultimate, and central outcome of all the work of God in this universe. Included with this tabernacle are justification in the outer court, sanctification in the Holy Place, and glorification in the Holy of Holies.

JUSTIFICATION, SANCTIFICATION, AND GLORIFICATION FOR THE BODY LIFE

The book of Romans also includes the steps of justification, sanctification, and glorification to meet the requirements of God's righteousness, holiness, and glory. The first step of justification is from Romans 1:1 to 5:11. This part of Romans tells us that we are sinful and under God's condemnation, but through the blood of Jesus, we have been justified. From 5:12 through 8:13 is sanctification and 8:14-39 talks about glorification. God first justifies us, and then He works to sanctify us. To be sanctified means to be mingled with God. The more you are mingled with God, the more you are sanctified. According to the picture of the tabernacle, all forty-eight boards were overlaid with gold. To be sanctified means to be overlaid by God and with God. God has not only justified us, but has also put us into Christ. God has identified us with Christ, has grafted us into Christ, and has made Christ one with us. We are now in Christ. In Romans 8 the Spirit is referred to as the Spirit of life (v. 2). Christ is the Spirit, and this Spirit is the Spirit of life. He is in you, you are in Him, and you have to learn to live not by yourself but by Him and in Him. To live by and in the Spirit of life is to be in the process of sanctification. Sanctification means to be mingled with the divine nature. Only Christ in His divine nature is holy. Romans 8:14-39 tells us that after we are justified and sanctified, we will be glorified.

Romans 9—11 is a parenthetical section which talks about God's selection. Chapters twelve through sixteen reveal the Body life. Thus, the book of Romans reveals the tabernacle of God. Justification through Christ's redemption is in the outer court, sanctification is in the Holy Place, and glorification is in the Holy of Holies. The church life is the mingling of the Triune God with His chosen people. The three stages of justification, sanctification, and glorification embody the church life, the Body life. The church life is the Triune God (God as the source embodied in Christ and realized as the Spirit) mingled with His chosen people. These chosen people are justified, sanctified, glorified, and built together to form the tabernacle, the Body, the church. This truth is the seed of all things related to God's purpose.

CHRIST AS THE SEED OF LIFE
BEING THE SEED OF THE KINGDOM,
THE CHURCH, THE CHRISTIAN LIVING,
AND THE CHRISTIAN MINISTRY

With God's purpose there is the kingdom, the church, the Christian living, walk, or conduct, and the Christian work, service, or ministry. With the kingdom of God, the church of Christ, the Christian living, and the Christian ministry, there is a seed. The seed of life is related to everything of God's purpose.

The Kingdom

Some Bible teachers refer to the matter of the kingdom merely as a dispensational truth. But we need to see that first in Matthew the kingdom is likened to a seed sown into the soil (Matt. 13:3; cf. Mark 4:26). This seed is Christ, the embodiment of the Triune God. How could this holy Christ as the very divine embodiment of God be sown into us when we were so sinful, so much related to Satan, and thoroughly, absolutely, involved with all the negative things in the universe? Before He came into us, this seed passed through death and resurrection. He prepared a place in the Father and paved the way for us to be brought into the Father. This seed has accomplished whatever was needed so that He could come into us. Out of this seed the kingdom will grow out.

In Matthew 13 there are seven parables related to the kingdom. In those seven parables, the seed is Christ sown into us to grow in us, and the enemy, Satan, comes in to do whatever he can to frustrate and to damage the growth of this seed. Satan's aim is to frustrate the growth of this seed because the growth of this seed will bring forth the kingdom. In Matthew 13 the seed is sown, and then it grows in the good earth to produce fruit. Also, in those seven parables a treasure hidden in the field (v. 44) and pearls are mentioned (vv. 45-46). These items signify the transformation of life. Thus, the kingdom is something of life and of the enjoyment of God as the tree of life for the transformation of life.

John 3:5 says, "Unless a man is born of water and the Spirit, he cannot enter into the kingdom of God." The kingdom of God is a matter of life. You have to partake of God as the tree of life to have a share in the kingdom of God. Our fellowship in this chapter shows that all the things related to God and to His purpose are a matter of the enjoyment of God as life. Even the kingdom of God is a matter of the enjoyment of God as the tree of life. From this life the kingdom of God will grow up and grow out. The seed of the kingdom is the very Triune God as the tree of life planted into us. The kingdom is the growth of the tree of life which has been planted into us. In Luke 17 the Lord Jesus told the Pharisees, "The kingdom of God is among you" (v. 21). The Lord Jesus revealed that the kingdom of God is the Savior Himself, who was among the Pharisees when He was questioned by them. The kingdom is the Lord among us and within us.

The Church

We need to see that the church is also the growth of the tree of life planted into us. The more we enjoy Christ as the tree of life, the more the element, the reality, of the church will be growing up. The more we grow in Christ, the more the church will come into existence. Thus, the church is the outcome of the tree of life growing within us.

The Christian Living

Now we need to consider what the Christian walk, the Christian living, is. Galatians 5:22 refers to the fruit of the Spirit, which is the outcome of the tree of life within us. This outcome of the tree of life within us is the Christian's daily walk or living. The Christian walk, Christian living, Christian conduct, Christian behavior, must not be a religious performance but must be something divine and spiritual, something of the Spirit of God.

When I was young, I was taught by the missionaries that Christianity was a religion of love, that we Christians had to love others. Some of the teachers in my school were students of Confucius. They compared the teachings of the Bible with the teachings of the classical book of Confucius. They said that the teachings of Confucius were much better, ethically speaking, than the teachings of the Bible, and they could prove it. It was hard to argue with their logical reasoning. I was very confused. As one who was born Chinese, I thought that there was no way for me to receive Christianity since the teachings of Confucius seemed to be better. When I got saved, I realized that no matter how good the teachings of Confucius were there was no thought of redemption in them. I like to take Christ because with Christ, there is the redeeming blood. Years later I realized further that with Christ there is not only the redeeming blood but also the divine life.

With the Christian walk, with the Christian living, with the Christian behavior, it is not merely a matter of proper conduct but even more a matter of life. As Christians we are not just to love people but we are to live Christ out as love. We are not just to be humble, but we are to live Christ out as humility. Polished brass may shine more than a piece of gold, but their natures are entirely different. We are not just outwardly loving others, showing humility to others, or being patient with others. We are living out Christ. Our behavior, our living, our conduct, our walk, must be the outcoming of Christ, the fruit of the Holy Spirit from within us. When the Holy Spirit lives in us and we live by Him, then some fruit will come forth, the fruit of the Spirit. This fruit is our Christian walk, our Christian behavior, and is something absolutely different from the teachings of Confucius.

Regardless of how good the teachings of Confucius are, they can never produce something divine and holy. They can never impart the holy, divine nature of God into you. But in our Christian walk, in our Christian living, there must be the divine nature. The Christian walk is not a kind of living corrected, adjusted, taught, and disciplined by the best teachings of the philosophers. The Christian living is something flowing out from within us by our taking Christ as life, by our living in the Holy Spirit. We have to give the seed of life, which has been sown into us, an opportunity to grow up and to grow out of us.

The Christian Ministry

Furthermore, the Christian service, the Christian ministry, must be the overflow of the inner life. We are not merely working, but our work is the overflow of the divine life from within us. The seed of the work, the seed of the ministry, the seed of the service, must be the all-inclusive Christ. If this Christ is the seed of our work, our Christian work will be revolutionized. The proper work is that first Christ has to be sown into us as a seed. Then we have to let Christ grow up and flow out. This outflowing of Christ is the work, the service, the ministry. The work is not a matter of how much we can do or accomplish, but a matter of how much of Christ we can live out, flow out.

Christ is the seed of the kingdom, the seed of the church, the seed of the Christian walk, and the seed of Christian service. Christ is the seed of everything related to God's purpose. Regardless of what gift we have or of what kind of gift we are to the Body, we have to realize that our work, our ministry, must be a work and ministry with Christ as the seed sown into us to grow up within us and to flow out from within us in order to minister Christ into others. May the Lord help us to realize what it means to have Christ as the seed in the kingdom, in our church life, in our daily walk, and in our work.

CHRIST AS THE SEED OF LIFE BEING THE
SEED OF EVERYTHING RELATED TO GOD'S PURPOSE

We need to look at a number of verses which show that Christ as the seed of life is the seed of everything related to God's purpose. Psalm 34:8 says, "O taste and see that the Lord is good." We have to taste the Lord, not only know Him. Then 1 Peter 2:2-3 says, "As newborn babes, long for the guileless milk of the word, that by it you may grow unto salvation, if you have tasted that the Lord is good." A mother gives milk to the newborn babes that they may grow. The best way to help the new believers to grow is to feed them. To merely teach is easy, but to feed is not so easy. The newborn babes need milk to drink that they may grow. The Lord can be tasted, and His taste is pleasant and good. If we have tasted Him, we will long for the nourishing milk in His word.

First Peter 3:7 says, "The husbands, in like manner, dwelling together with them [the wives] according to knowledge, assigning honor as to the weaker, female vessel, as also joint heirs of the grace of life." The grace of life is God as life and life supply to us in His Trinity—the Father as the source of life, the Son as the course of life, and the Spirit as the flow of life, flowing within us with the Son and the Father (1 John 5:11-12; John 7:38-39; Rev. 22:1). All believers are heirs of this grace. The grace of life is the tree of life, the Triune God. The weaker female vessels are joint heirs of the grace of life, the tree of life.

Second Peter 1:3-4 says, "As His divine power has granted to us all things which relate to life and godliness, through the full knowledge of Him who has called us to His own glory and virtue, through which He has granted to us precious and exceedingly great promises, that through these you might become partakers of the divine nature." Life is the seed; godliness is the fruit. Life is something within; godliness is something without. To be partakers of the divine nature is to be the eaters of the tree of life.

In Acts 5:20, an angel of the Lord told Peter, "Go and stand in the temple and speak to the people all the words of this life." What does "this life" mean? This was the life that Peter was enjoying. The angel told Peter to minister this life that he was enjoying to the people. This life is the divine life preached, ministered, and lived by Peter that overcame the Jewish leaders' persecution, threatening, and imprisonment. This word indicates that Peter's life and work made the divine life so real and present in his situation that even the angel saw it and pointed it out. The words of this life are not *logos* but *rhema*, the present, living, practical word. What Peter was charged to speak was not a doctrinal teaching but the present, living, and practical word concerning the life that he was enjoying.

Romans 5:10 says, "For if, while we were enemies, we were reconciled to God through the death of His Son, much more, having been reconciled, we shall be saved in His life." We have been reconciled by His death, and we shall be saved in His life. I have been reconciled to God through the death of Christ, but now I am in the process of being saved in His life. The first section of Romans talks about being reconciled by His death. The second section talks about being saved in His life, the resurrection life.

Romans 5:21 says, "That as sin reigned in death, so also grace might reign through righteousness unto eternal life through Jesus Christ our Lord." Grace reigns as a king that we may enjoy life eternal in a kingly way. This life again is the Triune God as the tree of life. In Romans 5—8 what is stressed is the tree of life. Romans 8:2 says, "For the law of the Spirit of life in Christ Jesus has freed me from the law of sin and of death." The Spirit of life is the Triune God as the tree of life. When we enjoy Him, we will realize the full salvation, the full deliverance. This tree of life, this Spirit of life, this life-giving Spirit, is the root, is the seed, is the reality, and is the central point of all the spiritual things, of all the things related to God's purpose. Thus, we all have to learn how to feed on this tree of life.

CHAPTER ELEVEN

HOW TO FEAST ON THE TREE OF LIFE THROUGH THE WORD

Scripture Reading: Matt. 15:21-28; 22:2; 1 Cor. 10:21; 11:24-26; Rev. 19:9; Psa. 23:5; John 6:63; 2 Cor. 3:6; 1 Cor. 15:45b; 2 Cor. 3:17; 2 Tim. 3:16; John 1:1; 4:24

We have pointed out that the tree of life, the matter of life, is the very seed, the very root, of all the things related to God's purpose, especially in four main areas. First, the inner life is the seed of the kingdom of God. The kingdom of God is something that grows up and grows out of this seed of the inner life. Second, the church life is the outcome of the inner life. Third, the Christian walk, the Christian living, is also the outflow of the inner life. The Christian behavior, the Christian conduct, is not just something of human morality, but it is something of divine expression. The divine life is in us, and we live by this divine life with the divine nature. Then we will have the outflow of the divine life. Thus, the Christian behavior, the Christian walk, is the very expression of the inner divine life and divine nature and is the fruit of the inner, indwelling Holy Spirit. It is not just something human. It must be divinity mingled with humanity. Fourth, the Christian work, the Christian service, or the Christian ministry is not just an activity but an overflow of the inner life. As we feed on the Lord Jesus, we will flow out something of Himself to minister to others.

THE CHILDREN'S BREAD

Matthew 15:21-28 records the Lord's contact with a Canaanite woman: "And Jesus went from there and departed into the parts of Tyre and Sidon. And behold, a Canaanite

woman came out from those regions and cried out, saying,
Have mercy on me, Lord, Son of David; my daughter is badly
demon-possessed! But He did not answer her a word. And His
disciples came and asked Him, saying, Send her away, for she
is crying out after us. But He answered and said, I was not
sent except to the lost sheep of the house of Israel. But she
came and worshipped Him, saying, Lord, help me! But He
answered and said, It is not good to take the children's bread
and throw it to the dogs. And she said, Yes, Lord; for even the
dogs eat of the crumbs which fall from their masters' table.
Then Jesus answered and said to her, O woman, your faith is
great; let it be done to you as you desire. And her daughter
was healed from that hour."

In this passage of Scripture the Lord revealed Himself to the
Canaanite woman as "the children's bread." The Canaanite
woman considered Him the Lord, a divine person, and the son
of David, a royal descendant, great and high to reign. But He
unveiled Himself to her as small pieces of bread, good for food.
We may cry to the Lord day by day, asking Him to do things for
us without any realization that He is the children's bread for us
to enjoy, for us to feed on. From now on I hope we would contact
the Lord every morning with the realization that He is the children's bread. We may be the Gentile dogs but "even the dogs eat
of the crumbs which fall from their masters' table" (v. 27). As
the heavenly king, the Lord rules over His people by feeding
them with Himself as bread. We can be the proper people in His
kingdom only by being nourished with Him as our food. To eat
Christ as our supply is the way to be the kingdom people in the
reality of the kingdom.

THE CHRISTIAN LIFE BEING A LIFE OF ENJOYMENT

The Beginning of the Christian Life—
a Marriage Feast

Matthew 22:2 says, "The kingdom of the heavens was likened to a man, a king, who made a marriage feast for his son."
The proper preaching of the gospel is to invite people to a wedding feast. The unsearchably rich Christ is a feast prepared by
God for man's enjoyment. The gospel is a wedding feast. When

we preach the gospel to people, appealing to people, inviting people to come, this means that we invite them to come to a feast, not just to come to repent with tears. The Lord might tell these pitiful sinners, "Don't weep with tears but rejoice. You are coming to a feast. You have come to enjoy Me." The sinners have come to enjoy the tree of life. We may have been saved for years, but we may not have had this kind of realization. When we come to the Lord Jesus, we come to feast on Him. We come to partake of a feast. The beginning of the Christian life is an enjoyment of a wedding feast.

The Continuation of the Christian Life— the Lord's Table

After we got saved, day by day and week after week we feast at the table. First Corinthians 10:21 says, "You cannot drink the cup of the Lord and the cup of demons; you cannot partake of the table of the Lord and of the table of demons." After we get saved we have to come to the Lord's table continually, at least once a week. Lord's day after Lord's day we come to a table. The real remembrance of the Lord is to partake of Him by eating and drinking Him. First Corinthians 11:24 says, "And having given thanks, He broke it and said, This is My body, which is for you; this do unto the remembrance of Me." The breaking of the bread is that we may eat it (Matt. 26:26). The real remembrance of the Lord is to take Him and eat Him. We do not remember the Lord by using our mind to think, to consider, to meditate on something about the Lord. But we remember Him by exercising our spirit to feed on Him. First Corinthians 11:25 continues, "This cup is the new covenant in My blood; this do, as often as you drink it, unto the remembrance of Me." Again, the real remembrance of the Lord is to eat Him and to drink Him.

At the beginning of the spiritual life, we came to a wedding feast. Then after we are saved, week after week, we have to come to a feast, the Lord's table. At the Lord's table we exercise our spirit to eat and drink the Lord, once more testifying and even proclaiming to the whole universe that this is the way that we live by the Lord. We live by taking Christ as our food and drink. We live by eating Him and by drinking

Him. This is the real remembrance. The Christian life started with a wedding feast and continues with the Lord's table until the Lord comes (1 Cor. 11:26).

The Consummation of the Christian Life— the Marriage Dinner of the Lamb

Revelation 19:9 says, "And he said to me, Write, Blessed are they who are invited to the marriage dinner of the Lamb." This is the time of the Lord's coming back. At the Lord's coming back, the overcoming believers will enjoy the marriage supper of the Lamb. At the marriage supper of the Lamb, the believers will enjoy a special portion of Christ. A wedding feast is not ordinary food but a special portion. The Lord Himself by that time will be a special portion for us to enjoy.

The Christian life starts with a wedding feast, continues with His table week after week until He comes, and at the time He comes, we will have a marriage supper. The entire Christian life from the beginning to the end is the enjoyment of a feast. Do we enjoy the Lord all the time in our Christian life? Do we feast and feast again and again in our Christian life? The Christian life is a life of feasting. It starts with feasting, continues with feasting, and ends with feasting. We will feast on the Lord eternally.

Instead of feasting on the Lord all day, it may be that we are striving. Even in the battlefield, however, the Lord prepares a table before us in the presence of our enemies (Psa. 23:5). While we are fighting, we are feasting. If we do not know how to feast, we could never fight properly. Only those who know how to feast on the Lord, know how to fight for the Lord. The Christian life is a life of enjoyment. In 1958 I was in a conference in Denmark. One day the leading brother there said, "Brother Lee, do you worry? To me you are always happy. Don't you have some troubles?" I do have troubles, but my secret is that I am a feasting Christian. In myself I should be sorrowful, but in Him there is a real feast. Try to be a feasting Christian, not a striving Christian.

We need to see that the Christian life is a feasting life. We are destined and ordained to feast on the Lord. When I was young, my pastor told me that we were appointed by God to suffer. That frightened me. Later on in my Christian life I found out that we all have to pass through sufferings, but we are destined and ordained by God to feast on Him. The beginning of the Christian life is a feast, the continuation of the Christian life is a table, and the consummation of the Christian life is an eternal feast. May the Lord be gracious to us so that we may begin to feast on Him day by day. Come to the table! Come and feast!

THE LORD BEING THE SPIRIT AND THE WORD

Now we come to the practical point of how to feast. According to the biblical revelation, the Lord is the Spirit and the living Word. John 6:63 and 2 Corinthians 3:6 tell us that it is the Spirit that gives life. Who is this Spirit? First Corinthians 15:45b says, "The last Adam became a life-giving Spirit," and 2 Corinthians 3:17 says, "The Lord is the Spirit." The Lord is the Spirit that gives life, and this life-giving Spirit is the incarnated, crucified, resurrected, and ascended Christ. Christ by His death and resurrection became a life-giving Spirit. As food to us, as a feast to us, Christ is the life-giving Spirit. Our food is the Spirit.

The Spirit is abstract like the air, but the Word is concrete. In John 6:63 the Lord also said, "The words which I have spoken unto you are spirit and are life." In our concept we always consider that the Word of God involves knowledge and teachings in letters. But the Lord tells us that His words are spirit. The word of the Lord is spirit. Second Timothy 3:16 says that "all Scripture is God-breathed." This indicates that the Scripture, the Word of God, is the breath of God. Hence His Word is spirit, *pneuma,* or breath.

We should not consider the Scripture to be merely in letters. The Scripture is the breath of life. The words spoken by the Lord are spirit because the Lord Himself is the Spirit. Thus, whatever is breathed out of Him must be spirit. We have to change our concept. The word does not equal knowledge but spirit. The words the Lord speaks to us are spirit, not knowledge, and all Scripture is the breath of God. The Lord Himself is in the Word, and He Himself is even called

the Word. In the beginning was the Word, the Word was God
(John 1:1), and God is Spirit (4:24). The Lord is the Word, and
the Word is the Spirit.

EXERCISING OUR SPIRIT TO TOUCH THE WORD

A newspaper is composed of material in black and white,
in letter only. When we read the newspaper, we must exercise
our eyes to read and our mind to understand. But we cannot
and should not deal with the Word of God in this way. The
Word of God needs our eyes to read, but it is not for our eyes
to read. It needs our mind to understand, but it is not for our
mind to understand. The eyes are the members of the physical body, and the mind is the main part of the soul. But the
Word is for our spirit to receive and digest. After we read and
understand the Word, we have to exercise our spirit to take
the Word. The Word is not for our eyes to read nor for our
mind to understand, but for our spirit to feed on. If we do not
exercise our spirit while reading the Word, the Bible is the
tree of knowledge to us and not the tree of life. The same
Bible may be a book of knowledge to one person or a book of
life to another person. Whether it is a book of knowledge or
a book of life depends on what organ we use to deal with this
book.

After I received the Lord as a young man, for at least
seven years I contacted the Bible without realizing I needed
to exercise my spirit to touch the Lord in the Word. No one
ever helped me to realize that I had to exercise my spirit to
deal with this spiritual book. I was never taught in this way.
Thus, the more I studied this book merely with my mind, the
more dead I became. The more I studied, the more I was filled
with dead letters, dead knowledge. We have to exercise our
spirit to deal with this living Word and to touch the Word.
Then the Word becomes spirit. When it becomes spirit, it
becomes life. When it becomes life, it is the food, the supply of
life, to us.

When we come to the Word, we have to read it with our
eyes and understand it with our mind, but there is no need
for us to exercise our mind too much. Our mind has been
over-exercised. Even when we are sleeping, our mind is still

exercised because we dream. If we do not understand something when we are reading the Word, we should not be bothered. After we understand something, however, we have to exercise our spirit to touch that portion of the Word by the way of prayer. Right away we have to pray about what we understand and pray with what we understand.

THE WRITTEN WORD BECOMING THE LIVING WORD

The Lord is the living Word, and the Bible is the written Word. Are the written Word and the living Word two kinds of words? If we consider the written Word to be something different from the living Word, the written Word will be dead knowledge to us. The written Word cannot be separated from the living Word but must be one with the living Word.

Many wives are very familiar with Ephesians 5:22 which says, "Wives, be subject to your own husbands as to the Lord." Most wives appreciate and respect others' husbands; hence, the apostle exhorts the wives to be subject to their own husbands as to the Lord, regardless of what kind of husbands they are. How could a wife transfer or translate this written word into the living Word? We have to realize that the submission to the husband which the wives should have is nothing less than Christ Himself. The wives should submit themselves to their husbands, and this submission is Christ.

After reading such a word, we have to put what we understand into prayer. A wife should not pray, "Lord, help me to submit myself to my own husband." The Lord never answers this prayer. She should pray, "Lord, I know that this submitting life, this submission, is You. I do not only take this word, but I also take You. Lord, work Yourself into me as this submitting life. Work Yourself into me to be my very submission. I take You as the reality of this word. I come to contact You through this word and in this word." If a wife prays in this way, she will enjoy the Lord. She may also pray, "Lord, I do not pay much attention to the matter of submitting, but I pay my full attention to You. I want to enjoy You. Lord, I thank You that You are so much to me. You are not only my Savior and my Lord but also my submission. My submission to my own husband is You Yourself. I am going to enjoy You and take You as my submission."

A wife could pray in the wrong way, "O Lord, You know I am weak. Lord, help me to submit myself to my husband." After this kind of prayer, you will be striving. You will be afraid of making a mistake with your husband and you will be on the alert all the time to make yourself so submissive. This is a real striving, not a feasting. In the morning a wife may endeavor to submit and be quite successful, but in the evening she will fail. Her experience is one of striving and failure. Then she may even feel too ashamed to pray. Maybe after two days she will come back to the Lord and repent—"Lord, forgive me. I failed. Lord, by Your mercy and Your grace, I make up my mind again to submit myself to my husband. Lord, You know how weak I am. Lord, help me." After this prayer, there will be striving and failure again.

If you learn to contact the Lord in the right way, it is not you that submits but the Lord. It is "no longer I who live, but Christ lives in me" (Gal. 2:20). It is no longer I but Christ as the submitting life. There is no need for me to endeavor or strive. I just need to feast on the Lord. After our prayer in the proper way to contact and enjoy the Lord as our submitting life, we will sing hallelujahs and praises to the Lord. We may even declare, "Hallelujah! I am in the Lord and I am in the heavens!" There is no need for us to make up our mind to submit ourselves. There is the inner grace ministering this submission into us when it is needed. Spontaneously and willingly we will submit with joy, with happiness, and with rejoicing. We will unconsciously submit ourselves. After we pray in a proper way, there is no tension. The wife will not pay attention to submitting, but she will appreciate and treasure her Lord Christ so much. After this kind of a time with the Lord, her face will become a shining face.

We have to deal with every verse of the Bible in this way. We read it by our eyes, understand it spontaneously by our mind, and deal with it by exercising the spirit to translate or transfer the written Word into the living Word, which is Christ Himself. Never pray in a way to ask the Lord to help you do something. That is the wrong way. Instead, always take Him as the fulfillment of His word. Suppose you read John 15:12, which says that we have to love one another. Do not pray, "Lord, I have to love my brother. But Lord, You know I am weak. Lord, help *me* to love." After this prayer you will make up your mind to love the brothers and you will be exposed and see the failure. You have to expect nothing but failure. You may be successful for a short time, but eventually you will fail. Even if you were successful, that would not mean anything nor would it be worth anything.

When we read this word—"love one another"—we have to take the word to the Lord by exercising our spirit to pray, "Lord, You are the love to love my brother. I just open to You. Lord, come in to fill me with Yourself as the love to love my brother. You are the loving life." We will eventually change our prayer into praise. "Lord, praise You. You are not only my life, but also my love." Thus, to love our brother is not a burden but a feast. It is not a suffering but an enjoyment. We enjoy the Lord when He is loving our brother through us. There is no need for us to make up our mind to love others. We just need to enjoy the Lord and the Lord will love others through us. We will love so much, yet we will love unconsciously.

The word of the Bible must be dealt with and taken in this way. Then we will really feed and feast on the Lord through the reading of the Word. Then the written Word will become the living Word, that is, Christ Himself. Christ and the Bible will be one. We need to taste and see. We have to help the brothers and sisters to contact the word of the Lord in this way. By the mercy of the Lord, we need to keep the Bible as a book of life, the tree of life, not as the tree of knowledge. Knowledge puffs up (1 Cor. 8:1). The more that many Christians learn the Bible, the more puffed up they become. They acquire knowledge just to condemn and to criticize others. Too much knowledge in dead letters results in pride. Do not make this living book a book of dead letters. Paul said that the letter kills (2 Cor. 3:6). That means that the Bible in the letter kills. We should not take the Bible as something in the letter. We have to take the Word as something in life and in the spirit. May we all taste and see that the Lord is good.

We have to change our way of reading this book. Always

remember that we have to read with our eyes, understand
with our mind, and receive and feed on the Word with our
spirit by praying. Then day by day we will be nourished. Day
by day the living Word will be made one with the written
Word, and day by day whenever we receive something of the
written Word it will become the Spirit. It is the Word before
us, but it will become the Spirit within us. When it becomes
the Spirit, it becomes life. The words the Lord speaks to us are
spirit and life. When the Word becomes the Spirit it is life, and
when it becomes life it is the life supply, the food, that nour-
ishes us.

There is a real need for us to spend some time to sit at the
table to feast on the Lord, to eat of the Lord, day by day. Then
we will be strengthened, refreshed, and nourished. Thus, we
will grow in life. We will not grow in dead knowledge, but
we will grow in life, in spirit, and with the stature of Christ. The
Lord is the tree of life. He presented Himself to us in the form of
food, and He is not only in the Word but He is also the Word
itself. We can contact Him by using our eyes to read the Word,
our mind to understand the Word, and our spirit to digest the
Word, to receive the Word, to take the Word in. We have to deal
with every portion of the Word by exercising our spirit. Then
the Word becomes living and becomes spirit and life. Then it is
our food. Day by day we have to feast on the Lord in this way.
May the Lord bring us into this life practice.

CHAPTER TWELVE

HOW TO FEAST ON THE TREE OF LIFE THROUGH PRAYER

Scripture Reading: James 5:17; Ezek. 1:16; Eph. 6:17-18; Matt. 6:33; John 17:1, 11, 25

THE DIVINE CONCEPT CONCERNING THE WORD OF GOD

Before we go on to see how to feed on the Lord and how to drink of the Lord by prayer, we need to see some more passages showing us what our concept should be regarding the Word of God. Our concept concerning the Word of God is that the Word is merely composed of teachings and instructions, but the divine concept concerning the Word of God is that the word from the Lord is food for us to feed on for our nourishment. Matthew 4:4 says, "Man shall not live on bread alone, but on every word that proceeds out through the mouth of God." The divine concept concerning God's Word is that it is food by which we are not only taught but also nourished. Jeremiah 15:16 says, "Thy words were found, and I did eat them." Jeremiah took the word as food to eat. First Corinthians 3:1-2a says, "And I, brothers, was not able to speak to you as to spiritual, but as to fleshy, as to infants in Christ. I gave you milk to drink, not solid food." The Apostle Paul's concept concerning the Word was that the Word was either milk or meat. Milk or meat is something for us to feed on in order to be nourished. Hebrews 5:12-14 says, "For when because of the time you ought to be teachers, you have need again for someone to teach you what are the rudiments of the beginning of the oracles of God, and have become those who have need of milk and not of solid food. For everyone who partakes of milk is inexperienced in the word of righteousness, for he is a babe; but solid food is for the mature, who because of practice have their faculties exercised for discriminating between both good and evil." The Word is nourishment as milk for the young ones and as solid food for the mature ones. First Peter 2:2 says, "As newborn babes, long for the guileless milk of the word, that by it you may grow unto salvation." All these passages confirm that we need our concept renewed concerning the Word of God. The natural concept concerning the Word is that it is a certain kind of teaching or doctrine, but the divine concept is that the Word of God is food to nourish our spirit.

Two passages from the Scripture show us that the Word is food to nourish us in the spirit. John 6:63 says, "The words which I have spoken unto you are spirit and are life." In Colossians 3:16 the infilling of spiritual life that overflows in praising and singing is related to the Word, whereas in its parallel passage, Ephesians 5:18-20, the infilling of spiritual life is related to the Spirit. This indicates that the Word and the Spirit are identical (John 6:63b). When we are filled with the Word, we are filled with the Spirit. It is rather hard for anyone to be filled with the Spirit without being filled with the Word. The Lord is the life-giving Spirit and the Word is also the Spirit. We have to deal with the Word as the Spirit and in our spirit. The Word as the Lord is spiritual food to feed our spirit. If we take the Word only into our soul, it becomes mere knowledge to us. But if we take the Word into our spirit and take it as the Spirit, the Word becomes our spiritual food. Whether the Word is mere knowledge to us or food depends on how we take it and depends on what part of our being we exercise to take it. We have to take the Word into our spirit by exercising our spirit. Then the Word will become life in us.

EXERCISING OUR SPIRIT TO CONTACT THE LIVING CHRIST AS THE REALITY OF THE WORD OF GOD

The Bible does teach us certain things, such as Ephesians 6:1 which says, "The children, obey your parents in the Lord, for this is right." Without the little phrase "in the Lord" or the phrase "in Christ" in other Scripture passages, the teaching of the Bible would be merely ethical and not divine. But the Bible is a divine teaching with the divine nature. "In the Lord" indicates to obey the parents: (1) by being one with the Lord; (2) not by yourselves but by the Lord; and (3) not according to your concept, but according to the Lord's word. The Bible says that the wives should be subject to their own husbands, but we must look at the context of this teaching in Ephesians 5. Verses 18 through 22 say, "And do not be drunk with wine, in which is dissipation, but be filled in spirit, speaking to one another in psalms and hymns and spiritual songs, singing and psalming with your heart to the Lord, giving thanks at all times for all things in the name of our Lord Jesus Christ to God and the Father; being subject to one another in the fear of Christ. Wives, be subject to your own husbands as to the Lord." A wife should submit to her husband in the condition of being filled in spirit and of being in the fear of Christ. We should not isolate the Word from the Spirit or from Christ. If the wives are to submit to their own husbands, they first have to be filled with the Holy Spirit, and then they have to be in the fear of Christ. Then Christ Himself will be the reality of their submission to their husbands. It will not be their doing, their behavior, their conduct, but it will be the overflow of Christ from within them. The reality of the Word of God is Christ as the Spirit. The Word should not be divorced or isolated from Christ. The Word is the very expression of Christ. Whenever we read the Bible, we have to receive it in the spirit as an expression of Christ in order to make Christ the reality of that word.

In 1 Timothy and Titus there are instructions regarding the eldership (1 Tim. 3:1-7; Titus 1:5-9). A careful reading of these books will bring one into the realization that the eldership can only be realized in the spirit by taking Christ as the reality of the eldership. The eldership is not a matter of the elders being merely good, moral, or ethical, but the eldership is something spiritual with Christ as the reality. The Word is the means to convey Christ to us. Without Christ as the content of the Word, the Word is empty to us. All the words in the Bible are means to convey Christ into us.

Whenever we come to contact the Word, to deal with the Word, we have to realize that the Word is the expression of

Christ, and we need to contact Christ in the spirit as the reality of the Word. Then the Word will not be divorced from the Lord or isolated from Christ. Then we will have the reality of the Word, which is Christ Himself. But we cannot do this by merely exercising our soul. The more we exercise our soul to contact the Word, the more we will isolate the Word from Christ. The problem with many Bible students is that they have isolated the Word from Christ by reading it merely in the mind or with the mind. When we read the Word, we will spontaneously understand something with our mind, but then we have to turn what we understand in our mind into the spirit by praying, by taking Christ as the reality of the Word. This is the proper way to take the Word. We all need to come back to Christ Himself, taking Christ as the reality of the Word in the spirit. What the Word conveys must be Christ. If the Word instructs us, the reality of that instruction is Christ Himself. The reality of submission is Christ. Even if one could submit on his own, that would not mean anything in the eyes of God. What God values is Christ Himself. Our submission must be Christ. Because the reality of all the instructions and teachings in the Word must be Christ Himself, we have to deal with the Word in the spirit, by the spirit, and through the spirit. Christ is the centrality and universality of all the things spoken by God in His Word, so we have to exercise our spirit to take Him as the reality in our spirit.

Let us forget about reading the Word merely for knowledge. Let us practice taking the Word as the expression of Christ and as the conveyer of Christ by exercising our spirit to contact the Word, taking the Word as Christ Himself and making Christ the reality of the Word. Then this Word will become our nourishment. The divisions among the Lord's children arose from the knowledge of the Bible in the letter. We all need to be delivered from the letter to the experience of Christ as the life-giving Spirit. We need a deliverance from the mere knowledge of letters to be brought back to the centrality, universality, and reality of the Word of God—the living Christ.

PRAYING IN THE SPIRIT WITH THE PRAYER OF CHRIST

We have to learn how to exercise our spirit to contact Chris as the life-giving Spirit by prayer. James 5:17 says, "Elijah was a man of like feeling with us, and in prayer he pra d that it should not rain, and it did not rain on the earth for hree years and six months." Many times we pray, but we do not pray in prayer or with prayer. There must be a prayer in our prayer just like the wheel within the wheel in Ezekiel 1:16. When we are going to preach the gospel we should be moving in the Lord's move. When we are ministering the Word, we should be ministering in the Lord's ministry. When we are praying, we should be praying with prayer. This means that when we pray, the Holy Spirit must be praying within our prayer. A prayer from the Lord was given to Elijah in which he prayed. He did not pray in his feeling, thought, intention, mood, or in any kind of motivation from circumstances or situations for the fulfilling of his purpose. He prayed in the prayer and with the prayer given him by the Lord for the accomplishing of God's will. Within our prayer, there must be a prayer of Christ. Andrew Murray said that the best prayer was one in which Christ prays within us to the Christ in the heavens. While we are praying, Christ must be praying within us.

Ephesians 6:18 tells us that we need to receive the Word of God "by means of all prayer and petition, praying at every time in spirit." The Lord is the Spirit, and we have to contact Him by praying in our spirit. He is the life-giving Spirit indwelling our spirit, so we have to exercise our spirit to pray. In our spirit there is another Spirit praying. Our spirit is the outer wheel and the divine Spirit in our spirit praying is the inner wheel. While we are praying by exercising our spirit, there is another One praying within our spirit, another Spirit. This Spirit is the life-giving Spirit, Christ Himself. The wheel within the wheel in Ezekiel 1 typifies the divine Spirit in our human spirit.

Some may ask how they could know that Christ is praying within them while they are praying. When one is eating some fruit, he may exclaim that it is delicious. If someone were to ask him how he knows it is delicious, he could only respond that what he is eating tastes delicious. We know that Christ is praying within us while we are praying because of the taste within. The more we pray with Christ's prayer, the more we are refreshed, the more we are watered, the more we are anointed, and the more we are strengthened. But sometimes when we pray, it is another story. When we do not pray with Christ's prayer, the more we pray, the more we are empty and dried up. When we pray without the prayer of Christ within us we are like a machine without oil. There is no smoothness in the machine's operation, and it will burn up due to the lack of oil. When we pray apart from Christ, we are exhausted. Prayer then becomes a real labor to us. This is because we are praying by ourselves and moving with an empty wheel. We may pray according to our mentality, our own inclination, our own emotions, and our own desires and not care for the Spirit in our spirit. Thus, the more we pray in this way, the more we are dried up with no watering, no anointing, no oiling, no refreshing, and no strengthening. We have to learn to drop this way of praying.

Matthew 6:33 says, "But seek first His kingdom and His righteousness, and all these things shall be added to you." When we pray we should not focus on our needs. Our Father knows all the things that we need and He will add these to us. We should leave our needs in His hands. He knows what we need better than we do. Husbands should not pray too much concerning their wives, and the wives should not pray too much concerning their husbands. In our prayer we have to take care of contacting the Lord Himself. We have to take care of honoring Him, praising Him, exalting Him, and glorifying Him. Then all our needs will be taken care of.

Many times in my prayer I simply did not have the liberty to pray for so many things. According to my intention, I wanted to pray for my relatives and for certain people, but when I knelt down to pray, something within me was going in another direction. Thus, I had to make a decision whether I would go along with my own direction to pray or pray according to His direction. If I prayed according to my own direction, the more I prayed, the more I would be dried up within. But if I forgot about my own direction and prayed according to His direction, the more I prayed, the more I would be refreshed and burning in spirit. Then the more I prayed, the more He prayed. This is the reality of the wheel within the wheel in Ezekiel 1. This is the way to pray in the Lord. By praying in the Lord we will be watered, refreshed, and strengthened. We will drink of the Lord, and our spirit will be open to Him by our prayer. By this kind of prayer, He has a way to flow out from within us. First, we will be watered, and then this water will flow out to others.

May we all be brought into the experience of Christ praying within us. We need to drive our "car" along the map given to us in this chapter. The best way for us to enjoy the Lord is to read the Word, realizing that He is the reality of the Word and taking Him, contacting Him, by exercising our spirit. Then we need to learn to pray in the spirit with Him praying in our prayer.

THE NEED TO LEARN THE PRINCIPLE OF PRAYER

We need to consider the prayer of the Lord in John 17 and the two prayers of the Apostle Paul in Ephesians (1:17-23; 3:14-19). We need to read these three prayers to learn the principle of prayer. This will help us to be brought into the realization of how the Lord prayed in the spirit and how the Apostle Paul prayed in the spirit. In John 17:1 the Lord prays to the Father, "Glorify Your Son that the Son may glorify You" (v. 1). The Lord began His prayer with God's glory from the Holy of Holies. In verse 11 the Lord addresses the Father as "Holy Father." This indicates that He has come out from the Holy of Holies to the Holy Place.

By the end of this prayer in verse 25 He calls the Father "Righteous Father." At the beginning of John 17 is the glorified Father, in the middle is the holy Father, and at the end is the righteous Father. This points to God's glory, His holiness, and His righteousness. The Lord started His prayer from the Holy of Holies and came through the Holy Place to the outer court in order to bring people into the Triune God.

The proper prayer must be started from the Holy of Holies, from the place where the glory of God is, from the place where the Father can glorify the Son and let the Son glorify Him. Then from this center where we start our prayer we can spread to the circumference, from the place of glory through the place of holiness to the place of righteousness to bring sinful people in by His righteousness and through His holiness to the place of His glory. We must learn how to pray from within the Holy of Holies by exercising our spirit to contact the Lord, passing through the Holy Place and coming to the outer court, the place of righteousness, to bring people into the Triune God. As we pray in this way, we will drink of Him, feed on Him, and breathe Him in to have a deeper mingling with Him, and we will be strengthened, nourished, and refreshed by Him. Let us learn to contact our wonderful Triune God in this way.

CHAPTER THIRTEEN

THE NEED TO BE POOR IN SPIRIT AND PURE IN HEART TO EXPERIENCE THE TREE OF LIFE

Scripture Reading: Ezek. 36:26-27; Matt. 5:3, 8; Heb. 4:12; Rom. 1:9; 7:6; 1 Pet. 3:4; Mark 12:30; 4:14-20; 2 Cor. 3:16-18; Jer. 31:33; Heb. 8:10; Psa. 51:6; Heb. 10:22

THE HEART AND THE SPIRIT

We want to see how we have to deal with our heart and our spirit in order to experience the tree of life. The heart and the spirit are referred to many times in both the Old and New Testaments. We need to be clear about the position and function of the heart and about the difference between the heart and the spirit. We need to come back to the pure Word to see the difference between the heart and the spirit.

Ezekiel 36:26-27 shows us that the heart is different from the spirit. Heart and spirit are not synonyms but are two different things. These verses say, "A new heart also will I give you, and a new spirit will I put within you...and I will put my Spirit within you." The new spirit mentioned here is not the Holy Spirit because in verse 27 there is another Spirit which will be put into us, into our spirit. The human heart is different from the human spirit. Both of these organs of our human being have to be renewed.

Matthew 5:3 says, "Blessed are the poor in spirit, for theirs is the kingdom of the heavens." The spirit referred to here is our human spirit, not the Holy Spirit. To be poor in spirit does not mean that one has a poor spirit. To be poor in spirit is to have the best spirit. It is not only to have a humble spirit, but also to be emptied in our spirit, in the depth of our being, not holding on to the old things of the old dispensation, but unloaded to receive the new things, the things of the kingdom of the heavens. Our spirit has to be emptied of many things. Human beings are filled with many things in their spirit. Now that we have turned to the Lord, we have to evacuate our spirit to be poor in spirit. Matthew 5:8 says, "Blessed are the pure in heart, for they shall see God." If the heart were synonymous with the human spirit, there would have been no need for the Lord to give these two different blessings in Matthew 5. Our heart has to be pure and our spirit has to be emptied. A pure heart and an empty spirit are the two main conditions for the nine blessings spoken by the Lord in Matthew 5.

Hebrews 4:12 says, "For the word of God is living and operative and sharper than any two-edged sword, and piercing even to the dividing of soul and spirit, both of joints and marrow, and able to discern the thoughts and intents of the heart." The soul and the spirit are two different entities just as the joints and marrow are. The heart is also another item. With the heart are the thoughts and intents. Again we see that there is a distinction between the heart and the spirit. Our spirit is the organ for us to contact God (John 4:24), while our heart is the organ for us to love God (Mark 12:30). Our spirit contacts, receives, contains, and experiences God. However, it requires our heart to love God first. In our heart is the mind with the thoughts and the will with the intents.

Romans 1:9 says, "For God is my witness, whom I serve in my spirit in the gospel of His Son." Romans 7:6 tells us that "we should serve as slaves in newness of spirit." To serve the Lord is something in the spirit. To love the Lord is something in the heart. The heart is for loving, and the spirit is for serving. We need to serve in newness of spirit and not in oldness of letter.

THE HIDDEN MAN OF THE HEART

First Peter 3:4 says, "But the hidden man of the heart, in the incorruptible adornment of a meek and quiet spirit, which in the sight of God is costly." In our heart there is a hidden

man. The hidden man of the heart is the meek and quiet
spirit. If a man is hidden in a house, it is obvious that the man
and the house are distinct entities. The spirit is hidden in the
heart and is the hidden man of the heart. The wives' adornment before God should be their inner being—the hidden man
of their heart, which is their spirit, in meekness and quietness. This is the incorruptible adornment in contrast with
the corruptible hair, gold, and garments (3:3). This spiritual
adornment is costly in the sight of God. A person may dress in
nice clothing which is the adornment of the outward man, yet
this person may have a proud spirit. Outwardly this person is
adorned, but inwardly there is no spiritual adornment. Peter
charged the sisters not to pay much attention to their outward
adornment but to take care of the hidden man of the heart,
which is a meek and quiet spirit. Our spirit should be adorned
with meekness and with quietness.

LOVING THE LORD WITH ALL OUR HEART

Mark 12:30 says, "And you shall love the Lord your God
from your whole heart, and from your whole soul, and from
your whole mind, and from your whole strength." The function of the heart is to love. The heart is a loving organ and we
are told to love the Lord our God with all our heart.

DEALING WITH THE HEART SO THAT
CHRIST CAN GROW WITHIN US

The parable of the sower in Mark 4 focuses attention on the
human heart. The human heart is the soil for the seed sown by
the Slave-Savior. Mark 4:14 says, "The sower sows the word."
The sower is Christ and the word is also Christ. This means
that the Lord Jesus came to sow Himself into us. He Himself is
both the sower and the seed of life. Verse 15 says, "And these
are those beside the way, where the word is sown; and when
they hear, immediately Satan comes and takes away the word
which has been sown in them." "Beside the way" is the place
close to the way. It is hardened by the traffic of the way, and it
is difficult for the seeds to penetrate it. This typifies a preoccupied heart, hardened by worldly traffic and not open to
understand, to comprehend, the word of the kingdom. The soil

should not be preoccupied by anything and must be absolutely open for the seed of life, but the wayside has been trodden too much by worldly traffic. This is the heart that has been preoccupied by many other things, thus becoming hardened. The wayside signifies a preoccupied heart.

Verses 16 and 17 say, "And likewise, these are those being sown on the rocky places, who when they hear the word, immediately receive it with joy, and they have no root in themselves, but last only for a time; then when affliction or persecution comes because of the word, immediately they are stumbled." The rocky places do not have much earth. This signifies a stony heart. There is some ground good for the seed, but this ground is too shallow. Underneath this ground are the rocks. It is rather hard for the seed to root deeply into a stony heart. Many times we may be willing to receive the word, but we only receive it superficially because there are some rocks in our heart. Thus, it is hard for Christ as the seed of life to root deeply in us.

Verses 18 and 19 say, "And others are those being sown into the thorns; these are those who have heard the word, and the anxieties of the age, and the deceitfulness of riches, and the desires concerning other things entering in choke the word, and it becomes unfruitful." Our desires concerning other things can choke the word. You may not think that the anxieties of the age or the deceitfulness of riches trouble you, but what about the desires concerning other things? Some may be desirous of a high position or a high degree. The anxieties of the age, the deceitfulness of riches, and the desires concerning other things choke the word and it becomes unfruitful.

Verse 20 says, "And those are the ones sown on the good earth, who hear the word and receive it and bear fruit, one thirty, and one sixty, and one a hundred." The good ground, the good heart, is a heart that is not hardened by worldly traffic, without hidden sins, without the anxiety of the age and the deceitfulness of riches, and without the desires concerning other things. Such a heart is pure, good, and right.

The Triune God, who is the tree of life, has imparted Himself into us to be our enjoyment. He is the seed of life sown into our heart. Our heart is like the soil, the earth. If the soil of our heart is the wayside, trodden by the world and preoccupied by many things, it becomes hardened. Our heart must be released from any preoccupation for the seed of life to be sown in it. Our heart may not be preoccupied but there may be hidden rocks in our heart. The rocks are hidden sins, personal desires, self-seeking, and self pity, which frustrate the seed from gaining root in the depth of the earth. We may seemingly be a good brother or a good sister and yet we are superficial with the Lord because of the rocks in our heart. Thus, it is impossible for the Lord as the seed of life to grow within us deeply. It is also possible for our heart to be full of thorns which are the cares of this age, the deceitfulness of money, and the desires concerning other things. Some people have their heart set on a better car. Even this desire can hinder and choke the word from becoming fruitful. The thorns frustrate and choke the growth of the seed.

If we are going to have the Lord as the seed of life grow within us to be our full enjoyment, we have to deal with our heart. We have to ask the Lord to be merciful to us. By His mercy we have to deal with all these negative things in our heart. We have to deal with the things preoccupying us, with the hidden rocks, with the cares of this age, the deceitfulness of money, and the desires for other things. Then our heart will be good, right, proper, released, and prepared for Christ as the seed of life to grow within us.

TURNING OUR HEART TO THE LORD

Second Corinthians 3:16-18 says, "But whenever it [the heart] turns to the Lord, the veil is taken away. And the Lord is the Spirit, and where the Spirit of the Lord is, there is freedom. And we all with unveiled face, beholding and reflecting as a mirror the glory of the Lord, are being transformed into the same image from glory to glory, even as from the Lord Spirit." We may talk about the Lord as the life-giving Spirit, but our enjoying and experiencing the Lord as such a living Spirit depends upon our heart being turned to Him. When our heart turns to the Lord, the veil is taken away. Actually, our turned-away heart is the veil. To turn our heart to the

Lord is to take away the veil. Our heart is the crucial factor in our enjoyment of the Lord as the life-giving Spirit and in our being transformed into the Lord's image. If we are going to enjoy the Lord as the living Spirit and be transformed by Him, we have to deal with our heart. Our heart has to be turned to the Lord.

THE PARTS OF MAN

First Thessalonians 5:23 strongly indicates that man is of three parts: spirit, soul, and body. There are many other passages in the Scriptures showing us that man is a tripartite being (see *The Parts of Man* published by Living Stream Ministry). The three parts of the soul are the mind, the knowing part (Psa. 13:2; 139:14), the emotion, the loving part (1 Sam. 18:1; S. S. 1:7), and the will, the deciding part (Job 7:15; 6:7). The mind is for us to think, to know, and to consider; the emotion is for us to love, to hate, to be happy, or to be sorrowful; and the will is for us to decide or to choose. The soul is the very person of a man.

The spirit also has three parts. These are the conscience (Rom. 9:1; cf. 8:16), fellowship (John 4:24; Rom. 1:9), and intuition (1 Cor. 2:11). The conscience is for us to discern right from wrong and either justifies or condemns us. The fellowship is for us to contact God and to commune with God. The intuition means to have a direct sense or feeling in our spirit, regardless of reason or circumstance. The intuition can directly sense the mind, the will, the heart of God. Many times this direct sense is against the knowledge of the mind and the emotion or the feeling in the soul.

The heart is a composition of all the parts of the soul plus one part of the spirit, the conscience. Thus, the heart is made up of the mind, the will, the emotion, and the conscience. Hebrews 4:12 talks about the thoughts and intents of the heart. The thoughts are in the mind and the intents relate to the will. Hebrews 10:22 tells us that our hearts need to be sprinkled from an evil conscience, and we have seen that we need to love the Lord with our whole heart. The shaded area in the following diagram illustrates the parts composing the heart.

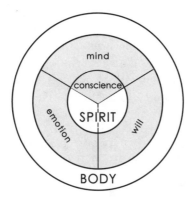

The above diagram shows us that the spirit is enclosed in the heart as the hidden man of the heart. Proverbs 4:23 tells us, "Keep thy heart with all diligence; for out of it are the issues of life." The heart is the gateway, the entrance and the exit of the spirit. When the heart is closed, the spirit is imprisoned. When the heart is open, the spirit will be released.

Jeremiah 31:33 says, "But this shall be the covenant that I will make with the house of Israel; After those days, saith the Lord, I will put my law in their inward parts, and write it in their hearts; and will be their God, and they shall be my people." We need to compare this verse with Hebrews 8:10. Hebrews 8:10 says, "I will impart My laws into their mind." In Jeremiah 31:33, inward parts is used for mind. This proves that the mind is one of the inward parts. It is also an interpretation of the term inward parts. The inward parts include not only the mind, but also the emotion and will, which are the composition of the heart. In Jeremiah 31:33 the Lord says He will put His law in our inward parts. But in Hebrews 8:10 the word "laws" is used. Eventually, the one law becomes many laws. By imparting His divine life into us, God puts the law of life into our spirit, from whence it spreads into our inward parts, such as our mind, emotion, and will, and becomes several laws. The law of life becomes a law of the mind, a law of the emotion, and a law of the will.

Psalm 51:6 says, "Behold, thou desirest truth in the inward parts: and in the hidden part thou shalt make me to know wisdom." Again, the inward parts are the mind, the emotion, and the will. Truth is something in the inward parts, and wisdom is something in the hidden part. Wisdom is deeper than truth. God desires that we would have truth in our mind, emotion, and will. In our spirit, which is the hidden part, the hidden man of the heart, He makes us to know wisdom.

OPENING OUR HEART TO THE LORD
BY REPENTING AND CONFESSING

We have seen that the Lord's intention is to sow Himself as the seed of life into us. We are the living earth, the living soil, the living ground. The spirit is enclosed by the heart, so if the Lord is going to come into us, our heart has to be opened. We can open our heart to the Lord by repenting and confessing. The word repent in the Greek language means to have a change of mind or a turn of mind. Our mind was originally not toward the Lord but toward something else, and our mind was fixed. Now we have to repent, which means we have to have a change of mind and we have to turn our mind. This means the mind is open to the Lord. Following our repentance, we will always confess. We need to confess all our failures, sins, and shortcomings to the Lord. Confession is the exercise of the conscience. When we repent by turning our mind, we will immediately confess by exercising our conscience. Then there is an opening of the heart. When we mean business to repent to the Lord and confess all our failures before God, our emotion will immediately be moved and touched. We will tell the Lord, "Lord Jesus, I love You." When our emotion is moved, our will makes a decision for the Lord. We will say, "Lord, from today I want nothing besides You. I want You to be my aim, my goal, and my one desire. I only want to seek after You." The mind of the heart turns, the conscience of the heart is opened, and the emotion and will of the heart follow. Thus, the whole heart is open to the Lord, and the Lord has a way to come into our heart. It is by repenting and confessing that we open our heart to the Lord. This is revealed in the Scriptures and proven by our experience.

The sad thing is that with many of us, soon after the Lord

came into us, we became closed to Him. Then the Lord was imprisoned in our spirit and had no way to make His home in our heart. After we got saved it may have been that gradually our emotion became closed to Him, our will became closed to Him, our mind became closed to Him, and our conscience became closed to Him. Thus, the Lord was imprisoned in our spirit. This is why both in the Old and New Testaments the Lord always calls us to repent. In the seven epistles to the churches in Revelation 2 and 3 the Lord tells the saints again and again to repent. Day by day and morning and evening we have to repent. To repent means to turn our mind to the Lord, to open our mind. Following this our conscience will be exercised in a thorough confession of our sins. Then our emotion will follow to love the Lord and our will will follow to choose the Lord. The result will be that our heart will be fully opened to the Lord, and the Lord will have a way to fill us with Himself. This is the way to deal with our heart to make it the good ground for the Lord as the seed of life to grow in.

If we deal with the Lord in this way, all our preoccupations will be rid from our being. The rocks and the thorns in our heart will be dealt with. Then our heart will be good and pure. The enemy is always looking for opportunities to make our heart the wayside. Many times we allow things to tread on the soil of our heart which make our heart hardened. We may be preoccupied by our wife, our children, or our parents. Sometimes we may be in a meeting listening to the word of God, but God's word cannot penetrate us. This is because our heart is preoccupied. Our heart can be preoccupied with earthly things, with things other than Christ Himself. We may feel that a brother or sister is really for the Lord, but we may not realize that their hearts contain some hidden rocks, thus making it impossible for the seed of life to take root within them. Also, the thorns, which are the cares of this age, the deceitfulness of riches, and the desires of other things, can grow together with the seed and choke the growth. The Lord is ready and available, but our heart is not so available. Our heart is not pure. This is why we have to deal with our heart. The heart has to be purified.

Hebrews 10:22 tells us that our hearts need to be sprinkled

from an evil conscience. We must have a conscience without any accusation or offense. Our conscience has to be cleansed and purged. Then our heart will be released from every preoccupying thing to be the good soil for the Lord Himself. All four parts of our heart have to be dealt with. The mind must be always turned to the Lord. The emotion must be always loving the Lord and fervent, zealous, for the Lord. The will must be submissive and pliable yet strong. Finally, the conscience must be purged and must be without any offense. Then we will have a proper heart. We must try to learn these lessons in life and help the children of God learn all these lessons. These are the necessary lessons for us to enjoy the Lord.

DEALING WITH THE LORD TO BE POOR IN SPIRIT

Besides dealing with the Lord to be pure in heart, we need to go on even deeper to be those who are poor in spirit. It may be that our spirit is not empty for something more of the Lord to be deposited into us. According to Matthew 5 we have to deal with our spirit first. The first condition for the nine blessings in Matthew 5 is to be poor in spirit. We need to pray, "O Lord, empty me. Evacuate and empty my spirit of anything other than Yourself. Even empty my spirit of the old experiences of Yourself." We should not be filled up with our old experiences of Christ. Our old experiences of Christ can hinder us from experiencing Christ in a new, fresh, and up-to-date way. Our spirit has to be emptied. This is the real humility. It is possible for a person to be humble outwardly, yet still be so proud in his spirit. The real humility is a matter in the spirit. This is why Peter tells us that there is the need for a meek and quiet spirit. The real meekness is in the spirit. A person may be quiet outwardly but may be full of opinions inwardly.

Day by day, we have to learn the lesson to deal with the Lord to be poor in spirit by emptying our spirit of many old things such as old knowledge and old experience. If our heart is not open, the Lord has no possibility to dispense Himself into us. If our spirit is full, the Lord also has no way to impart something fresh of Himself into our being. We have to be poor in spirit and pure in heart. We need to ask the

Lord to empty our spirit and clear up our heart. Then the Lord will have the free way in us and the adequate room in our being to fill us.

A PROPER HEART AND A PROPER SPIRIT
TO EXPERIENCE AND ENJOY CHRIST
AS THE TREE OF LIFE

The heart acts in cooperation with the spirit, but the spirit is the organ for us to directly receive and contact the Lord. If we are going to contact the Lord, we must exercise our spirit. If we are going to serve the Lord, we must exercise our spirit. If we are going to receive the Lord, to take the Lord in, we must exercise our spirit. But the exercise of our spirit depends on the condition of the heart. If the condition of our heart is wrong, it is hard for us to exercise our spirit. One thing we should never do with the saints in the church is to play politics. We should not have two faces, pretending to be one way to a brother's face, but undermining him behind his back. Our heart must be honest and sincere for us to experience the Lord. We have to be faithful, honest, and frank. If we feel that something needs to be said, we should say it faithfully, honestly, and properly. We are the children of God, the children in light. Our heart must be honest and pure. Our conscience must be purged. If our heart is condemning us, how can we pray in a proper way?

We all need to look to the Lord that we would learn the lesson of dealing with all these negative things in our being. We need to ask the Lord to grant us a pure heart with a mind that always turns to Him and that is set upon Him. We need to ask the Lord to grant us a conscience that is always exercised to confess our failures and our sins before Him. Then the Lord will have the way to make our emotion so fervent and zealous for Him with a will that is submissive, pliable, and strong. May we also deal with the Lord to be poor in spirit. We need to be hungry and thirsty for more fresh, new, and up-to-date experiences of the Lord. We should not be settled or fixed but be emptied in our spirit all the time. Then we will experience and enjoy Christ, and He will have the opportunity, the capacity, and the space to grow within us.

May the Lord grant us a proper heart and a proper spirit for us to experience and enjoy Him as the tree of life.

CHAPTER FOURTEEN

GOD'S INTENTION
FULFILLED IN TRANSFORMATION

Scripture Reading: Gen. 2:8-12; 1 Cor. 3:9, 12; John 1:42;
Heb. 12:2; 2 Cor. 3:18; Rev. 22:1-2; 21:18-21

As we have seen, the tree of life is the central subject, the central thought, of the entire Scripture. In the beginning God created the universe and He created man as a vessel to contain Him. Man was made as a container in order to have God as his contents. Thus, after God created man, He put man in front of the tree of life, which signifies the Triune God to be our life, our enjoyment, and our everything. God presented Himself to man as man's enjoyment that man may take Him in. By man's eating of the tree of life, the very Triune God could come into man and mingle Himself with man to make Himself one with man. First Corinthians 6:17 tells us that we human beings can be joined to the Lord as one spirit. We can be one spirit with the Creator, with God Himself!

God presented Himself as enjoyment to man but man fell. Thus, God changed His form from the tree of life to a redeeming Lamb. In the redeeming Lamb, God presented Himself to fallen man as life and everything. Through the redeeming Lamb, fallen man could be brought back to enjoy God as his life. Our second birth, the birth in our spirit (John 3:6), brought God Himself into us as our very life. After our birth we continue to enjoy Christ, the embodiment of the Triune God, as our food, our drink, our air, and even as our abode, our dwelling place, day by day. Thus, Christ becomes everything to us.

ENJOYING THE LORD AS
THE TREE OF LIFE AND THE FLOW OF LIFE
TO BE TRANSFORMED INTO THE IMAGE OF CHRIST

The tree of life signifies God in the Son as the Spirit to be

our life and everything. Genesis 2 records that God placed
man in front of the tree of life and that this man was a vessel
of clay (vv. 8-9). A river went out of Eden to water the garden,
and this river was divided into four heads (v. 10). The issue of
the flow of this river was gold, bdellium (a kind of pearl), and
onyx stone (v. 12). We need to look to the Lord that He would
give us a heavenly, spiritual view of this picture presented to
us in Genesis 2. We all need to be transformed from men of
clay, vessels of clay, into precious materials for God's building—gold, bdellium, and precious stones. If we are going to be
transformed from clay into precious material for God's building, we have to eat the fruit of the tree of life. If we eat the
fruit of the tree of life, this life becomes the pure, heavenly,
living, and spiritual water flowing within us. This flow of life
will transform the clay into gold, pearl, and precious stones.
All these precious materials are for God's building. The conclusion of the divine revelation shows us a city built of gold,
pearls, and precious stones (Rev. 21:19-21). When we enjoy
the Lord as the tree of life, this life flows within us and transforms us into the image of Christ.

GROWING IN LIFE FOR GOD'S BUILDING

The Apostle Paul tells us in 1 Corinthians 3 that we are
God's farm, God's building (v. 9). The building of God's temple,
God's dwelling place, is only possible by the growth in life.
This is why the farm is mentioned first and then the building.
The growth of life makes the building possible. Paul tells us
that the apostles are God's fellow-workers, God's co-workers,
who labor on God's farm to plant and to water. On the one
hand, the apostles are the farmers, the husbandmen, and on
the other hand, they are the builders. The planting and the
watering are so that we may grow in the divine life. Out of this
growth we become the proper materials for the building up of
the church, which are gold, silver, and precious stones (1 Cor.
3:12). In Genesis the second material is pearl while in 1 Corinthians it is silver. The Apostle Paul mentions silver instead of
pearl because in Genesis 2 sin had not entered yet and there
was no need of redemption. Silver signifies the redeeming
Christ with all the virtues and attributes of His person and

work. When Paul wrote 1 Corinthians 3 there was the real need of silver, the redeeming Christ.

HOW WE CAN BE TRANSFORMED
INTO PRECIOUS MATERIALS FOR GOD'S BUILDING

Now we need to go on to see how human beings of clay can be transformed into gold, silver, and precious stones for God's building. Peter was originally a man of clay named Simon. When he was brought to the Lord for the first time the Lord changed his name to Peter, which means a stone (John 1:42). Genesis 2 indicates that man was made from the dust of the ground, but the Lord called Simon a stone. The Lord changed Simon's name to Peter because when Peter began to know the Lord as the Son of God, as the living Christ, Peter had received the Lord into him. At that time a metabolic change took place within Peter. When Christ as the divine life is added into us some spiritual chemistry takes place and there is a metabolic change in our being. The clay is changed into a stone. Eventually, this stone will be transformed into precious stone, transparent and shining.

In the church we can have the heavenly, spiritual gold, silver, and precious stones by Christ as life transforming us. The more that we enjoy Christ, the more that we take Him in by eating Him, drinking Him, and breathing Him in, the more His life will transform us. The Christian life is not a matter of outward correction or adjustment but a matter of transformation, of a metabolic change in our inward being.

When I was a young Christian, I received a number of teachings concerning holiness and sanctification. The Brethren teaching tells us that sanctification is something positional. They point out the Lord Jesus' word in Matthew 23 to the Pharisees that it is the temple which sanctifies the gold (v. 17) and the altar which sanctifies the gift (v. 19). This makes the gold holy positionally by changing its position from a common place to a holy place. They also point out that the common food that we buy becomes sanctified through the word of God and our prayer (1 Tim. 4:5). This sanctification is positional. Another school stresses holiness as an eradication of the sinful nature. We must realize that the real holiness, the real sanctification, is not something merely positional nor is it an eradication of our sinful nature. Sanctification is not only a matter of position but also a matter of disposition, that is, a matter of being transformed from the natural disposition into a spiritual one. Sanctification is to work God's holiness into us by having God's divine nature imparted into our being. In this sanctification, Christ, as the life-giving Spirit, is saturating all the inward parts of our being with God's divine nature for our transformation in life.

There may be a certain sister in the Lord who loves the Lord very much, yet in her character, her disposition, there is the problem of a bad temper. She may be helped to realize that she has been positionally sanctified, that her position has changed in Christ. Formerly she was in Adam and now she is in Christ. She exercises to take this standing with the realization that she has been transferred out of Adam and into Christ. Because she is in Christ, she must be holy. But eventually this dear sister will discover that it does not work just to have the realization that she is positionally sanctified. Even though she realizes that she is in Christ, this does not stop her from losing her temper.

Other Christians believe that sanctification is the eradication of our sinful nature. There was a preacher in Shanghai many years ago who taught strongly the concept of eradication. He told people that they could not sin after they were saved. One day, this preacher and several young men who were under his teaching went to the city park in Shanghai. That park required the proof of a ticket in order to be admitted. This man bought three or four tickets to be used by a total of five persons. How did he do this? First some of them entered the park with the tickets. Then one of them came out with the tickets and gave a ticket to one of the others. This continued until all five men had entered the park. In this sinful way that preacher brought his four young disciples through the gate of the park. As a result of this, one of the young men began to doubt the teaching of eradication. He said within himself, "What are you doing? You say that sin has been eradicated from you. What is this?" Eventually the young man went to the preacher and said, "Was that not a sin?" The preacher replied, "No, that was not a sin. That was just a little weakness." The leader of this group who proclaimed that his sinful nature had been eradicated was wrong. We should never accept a teaching that says that we have become so spiritual and holy that it is impossible for us to sin. If we accept such a doctrine, we will be deceived, and the result will be misery.

Now that we have received Christ into us, we have to enjoy Him in the spirit day by day. We have to eat Him, drink Him, and breathe Him in. This living Christ within us will transform us and sanctify us in our disposition through our enjoyment of Him. For us to merely stand on the fact that we have been positionally sanctified and then endeavor to do something to stand against the sinful nature within us does not work. We need to realize that the living, life-giving Spirit, Christ as life, is within us. Now we need to open ourselves to Him day by day and even hour by hour. We need to eat Him, drink Him, breathe Him, and abide in Him to enjoy Him. Then He will transform us. This transformation is not an outward correction or adjustment. By enjoying Christ as life and by being filled with Him as life, His life swallows up all the negative things in our being. His life will swallow up our bad temper. His life will transform the clay vessels into gold, pearl, and precious stones.

Do not try to overcome your temper by your own effort. Your temper is too big for you to overcome by yourself. Do not deal with your temper but deal with Christ. Eat of Him as the tree of life. Rest under His shadow and enjoy His fruit. The life of Christ is living and powerful and can swallow up all the death and negative things within us. He will not only correct us, adjust us, deliver us, and save us, but He will transform us. We need to forget about our temper, our weaknesses, our problems, and our troubles. We need to take our eyes away from all these things and look to Christ. Look away from everything unto Jesus (Heb. 12:2), and set your mind upon Him (Rom. 8:6). Feast on Him, drink Him, breathe Him in, abide in Him, praise Him, adore Him, and behold Him. We need to be like a mirror beholding and reflecting the glory of the Lord (2 Cor. 3:18). When we behold the Lord in this way,

He infuses us with the elements of what He is and what He has done. Thus, we are being metabolically transformed into His image and all the negative things within our being are swallowed up.

To enjoy the Lord is the way of salvation, sanctification, and transformation. The more we are sanctified, the more we will be transformed and the more holy we will become. Our holiness will not just be a change in position but a change in our very nature. When we are being transformed, we are in resurrection and ascension. We are in a transcendent condition and all things are under our feet. Teaching people to correct themselves, to adjust themselves, or to improve themselves is not the right way, the heavenly way, or the divine way. The divine way is not self-correction, self-adjustment, or self-improvement. God's way is to put Christ into us for us to enjoy Him by eating Him, drinking Him, breathing Him in, abiding in Him, and letting Him be everything to us. He is living and powerful, and He will transform us. Transformation is much better than outward correction, adjustment, or improvement. Transformation is a heavenly, spiritual, divine metabolic change in our being. The Lord is transforming us from one degree of glory to another degree of glory. We are being changed from clay to gold, pearl, and precious stones. The way of transformation is to enjoy the Lord, to feast on Him. Transformation is a feast, an enjoyment.

All of us are like Mephibosheth, the grandson of King Saul (2 Sam. 4:4). Mephibosheth was lame; he was unable to walk. King David preserved his life, restored to him all his inheritance, and invited him to feast with him at the same table (2 Sam. 9:1-13). After Mephibosheth received grace from David, he only looked at the riches on David's table; he did not look at his two lame legs underneath the table. Whenever we look at ourselves, we discover that we are lame and we become discouraged. After we have been saved, we should forget about our two lame legs, and sit at the table of our King, Jesus Christ, to enjoy Him with all His unsearchable riches. We should only look at the riches on the Lord's table and enjoy them. By our enjoyment of the unsearchably rich Christ, He will transform us.

GOD'S ULTIMATE INTENTION FULFILLED
BY THE ENJOYMENT OF THE TRIUNE GOD
AS THE TREE OF LIFE

The precious materials at the flow of the river in Genesis 2 are for God's building. At the end of the divine revelation there are the tree of life, the river of water of life, and the precious materials built up as a holy city, the New Jerusalem (Rev. 22:1-2; 21:18-21). This city is the counterpart of Christ and the dwelling place of God for God to rest in. As the counterpart of Christ, the holy city satisfies Christ, and as the dwelling place of God, the holy city satisfies God.

The beginning of the Scriptures shows us the tree of life with a flowing river issuing in precious materials. At the end of the Scriptures there is a universal city built up with these precious materials with the tree of life growing in it and the river of life flowing in it. This shows that God's eternal purpose, His ultimate intention, is to have a divine building built by the tree of life with the flow of the river of water of life to produce the precious materials. According to God's ultimate and eternal intention we have to be transformed and built up. Transformation is for God's building. How spiritual we are depends on how much we have been transformed and how much we have been built up.

The book of Romans provides a sketch of the Christian life. This book begins with justification by faith (3:21—5:11) and continues with sanctification (5:12—8:13), transformation (12:1—15:13), conformation, and glorification (8:14-39) for the Body life (12:1-21). Through the Lord's redemption we are justified and brought back to Him. Now a transforming work is going on within us in the spirit. We have to be sanctified, transformed, and conformed to the image of the Son of God. This is all for the Body of Christ, which is the building. Justification is for sanctification, sanctification is for transformation, and transformation is for God's building. We are transformed and thus conformed into the very image of Christ that we may be materials good for God's building.

God's building is the expression of God Himself. The New Jerusalem has the appearance of jasper (Rev. 21:11) and jasper is also the appearance of God (4:3). The city's wall and the first foundation of the city are built with jasper (21:18-19). This means that with the New Jerusalem there is the image of God. Furthermore, within the holy city is the throne of God and the Lamb (22:1), which means that God's authority is exercised there. Thus, God's purpose and intention are fulfilled by the enjoyment of the Triune God as the tree of life.

I hope that we can bring this fellowship to the Lord in prayer so that this truth will be so living within us. Our need is to take Christ as our food, drink, air, and abode. Our need is to enjoy Him so that we may be transformed day by day and be built up together with others. Then God's image will be expressed among us and through us, and His authority will be exercised among us over the enemy. Thus, God's intention will be fulfilled.

CHAPTER FIFTEEN

LIVING LETTERS OF CHRIST BY BEHOLDING AND REFLECTING HIS GLORY

Scripture Reading: 2 Cor. 3:3, 6, 17-18

GOD'S INTENTION TO MINGLE HIMSELF WITH US

In the Scriptures a wonderful, mysterious, and glorious fact is revealed, that is, God's intention is to mingle Himself with us human beings. This glorious, mysterious, and wonderful fact is the very central thought revealed in the Scriptures. The first illustration of God's intention in the Scriptures is the tree of life, which is to be taken as food into our being. The tree of life typifies the Triune God with the Father as the source, the Son as the course, and the Spirit as the flow that we may partake of Him as our food. He is presented to us in the form of food that we may take Him in. Then He will be mingled with us. The best way to have something mingled with us is to eat that thing. In order to have a chicken mingled with our being, we have to eat the chicken. When we eat chicken, it becomes a part of our being, our very constituent. When we eat the Lord as the tree of life, He will be one with us and He will be mingled with us.

Another illustration in the holy Scriptures is the lamb (Exo. 12:3-4; John 1:29). Most Bible students know that the lamb is for redeeming. During the Passover, the children of Israel slew the lamb, and the blood of the lamb was shed for their redemption. Under the covering of the sprinkled blood of the lamb, the children of Israel enjoyed the lamb by eating it. They feasted on the meat of the lamb. After a short time the entire lamb got into the children of Israel, who had been feasting on the lamb. On the evening of the Passover, every home had a lamb, but within a short time all these lambs disappeared. They became one with the children of Israel. This illustrates that the lamb was mingled with the children of Israel.

There are two illustrations in 2 Corinthians 3 that also illustrate God's heart's desire to mingle Himself with us. Verse 3 of this chapter says, "Being manifested that you are a letter of Christ ministered by us, inscribed not with ink, but with the Spirit of the living God; not in tablets of stone, but in fleshy tablets of the heart." The first illustration is that we are the letters of Christ inscribed with the Spirit of the living God on our hearts. Second Corinthians 3:18 says, "And we all with unveiled face, beholding and reflecting as a mirror the glory of the Lord, are being transformed into the same image from glory to glory, even as from the Lord Spirit." The second illustration in 2 Corinthians 3 is that we are mirrors beholding and reflecting the glory of the Lord. These two illustrations show that God wants to mingle Himself with us.

LIVING LETTERS OF CHRIST

When ink is applied to paper, it is mingled with the paper. Christ Himself desires to be inscribed into our being so that we can become living letters of Christ. A letter of Christ is one composed of Christ as the content to convey and express Christ. All believers of Christ should be such a living letter of Christ, that others may read and know Christ in their being. Our heart, as the composition of our conscience (the leading part of our spirit), mind, emotion, and will, is the tablet upon which the living letters of Christ are written with the living Spirit of God. This implies that Christ is written into every part of our inner being with the Spirit of the living God to make us His living letters that He may be expressed and read by others in us.

Christ desires to be written into every part of our inner being, our heart, but we may be preoccupied by many other things. How can Christ be written into us and written on our heart when our heart is preoccupied with other things? Our heart may be preoccupied with our family, our material possessions, our education, our job, or our future expectations. There are many things that can usurp the place of Christ in our heart. How many preoccupations are in our heart, giving no room for Christ to write Himself into us? Furthermore, our heart may be closed to Christ. The preoccupations of our heart and the closing of our heart have to be dealt with. The filthiness, the uncleanness, of our heart also needs to be dealt with. Is our mind pure? Is our emotion clean? Is our will right? We all have to confess that to one degree or another there is dirt in our mind, emotion, and will. Although we may come to the church meetings, we need to ask ourselves how much of Christ has been written into us. There may be no possibility, no ground, no opportunity, for the Lord to come in to write Himself into us because our heart is preoccupied with other things, closed to the Lord, and dirty, impure.

By the Lord's mercy, we need to open our being to Him. When we open our heart to Him, He gets in. He is waiting for us to open to Him so that He can write Himself into our inner being. We need to ask ourselves what our situation, condition, and relationship are with the Lord.

We have seen that the spirit is the very inmost part of our being, the hidden man of the heart (1 Pet. 3:4). Christ as the life-giving Spirit has come into our spirit to make us alive, to regenerate us, to indwell us. Christ lives in our spirit (2 Tim. 4:22). Ezekiel 36:26 shows us that the heart and the spirit are two things. God gives us a new heart and a new spirit. The heart is composed of the mind, the will, the emotion, and the conscience. The Lord wants to inscribe Himself as the Spirit into our heart, "in fleshy tablets of the heart" (2 Cor. 3:3). As the letters of Christ we are to express Christ. The letter is an expression. Thus, this letter is not written on our spirit but on our heart that Christ might be expressed and be read by others. A person expresses himself by his mind, emotion, and will. If Christ is written only on our spirit, He will be hidden; He will not be seen, read, or expressed. Christ as the living Spirit must be written on our heart, which includes our mind, emotion, and will, so that He can be expressed and be seen by others.

Christ is in our spirit as the life-giving Spirit, and as the Spirit He is the heavenly ink to be inscribed, to be written, on our heart, which includes the mind, the emotion, and the will.

This means that Christ will be mingled with our mind, emotion, and will. Then in our mind there will be the description of Christ, in our emotion there will be the definition, the explanation of Christ, and in our will there will be the expression of Christ. Then when people look at our mind, emotion, and will, they will see Christ. A wife's love for her husband should be full of Christ. Her emotion should be describing Christ, expressing Christ.

We are the letters of Christ written by the living Spirit of the living God on our heart. People should be able to read Christ in our being, in what we are. When we think, love, and make decisions, there should be the expression of Christ. When people notice our thoughts, our desires, our love, our hatred, the decisions that we make, and what we choose, they should be able to read something of Christ. For Christ as the Spirit of the living God to be inscribed into our being is for Him to mingle Himself with us. Christ is within us, but how much of Christ has been written into our mind, emotion, and will? It may be that our heart is preoccupied. We may listen to the ministry of the word and get nothing because we are preoccupied.

On the one hand, it is easy to be disappointed when you look at the situation among the Lord's children. Many Christians' hearts are indifferent toward the Lord and the Lord has gained very little ground within them. On the other hand, I am still joyful because the Lord is so gracious, patient, and merciful. The Lord is continually waiting for chances to mingle Himself with us. Whenever we call on His name, He takes the opportunity to mingle Himself with us a little bit. I have the assurance that sooner or later we will be transformed. If we are not transformed in this age, we will eventually be in the next age. The Lord is sovereign and no one can stop Him from accomplishing His eternal purpose. His enemy may be able to frustrate Him a little bit, but this frustration gives Him an opportunity to display His multifarious wisdom (Eph. 3:10). The Lord will accomplish His purpose. He has chosen us and we cannot retreat. He has called us, justified us, saved us, regenerated us, and has indwelt us. Even if we wanted to divorce Him, He would not sign the divorce papers.

Sooner or later you will be subdued, convinced, taken over, occupied, and transformed by the Lord. Regardless of how much you love the world today, how much you are indifferent to the Lord, how cold your emotion is, and how stiff-necked your will is, I know that one day you will be absolutely gained by the Lord. He is merciful and He is waiting. He has been waiting for two thousand years. We may feel that two thousand years are too long, but to Him one thousand years are just one day. One day He will purify us and clear us up. Today the Lord is within our spirit and He is always waiting for opportunities to dispense Himself into us, to occupy our heart little by little. The all-inclusive, rich Christ is within us as the living Spirit. He is the heavenly ink waiting to inscribe Himself on the fleshy tablets of our heart. Whenever we turn to Him, the living Spirit will write something of Christ upon our mind, emotion, and will.

The Lord's main concern is not for what we do outwardly but for what we are. He wants to dispense Himself, inscribe Himself, into our mind, emotion, and will all the time. One brother may be very good in his natural disposition. He may be nice, humble, and very stable. Since he got saved, he is so nice and humble all the time and everyone likes him. He even comes to the church meetings on a regular basis. But it may be that this brother is always closed to the Lord. The Lord is within his spirit as a prisoner. Outwardly he is such a nice brother, and he is really stable. But the Lord has no way to write on his heart because he is not open to the Lord.

There may be another brother who is not good in his natural disposition. Right after he got saved, he may have backslidden. Then he came back to the Lord and confessed his sins, opening his heart to the Lord. This gave the Lord a chance to write on his being. Maybe a little later this brother had a fight with some other brothers. Then he repented and realized he was wrong. He confessed to the Lord and opened his heart again, so the Lord dispensed more of Himself into this brother. We have to consider where these brothers will be after fifteen years with the Lord. The one brother is so nice, humble, and stable, but always closed to the Lord. The other brother is not good according to his natural disposition, but gradually more and more of

Christ has been wrought into him. The Christ that has been wrought into him will gradually swallow up his bad disposition and there will be a real transformation with this brother. This shows us that the Christian life is not a life of outward doing, of outward working, but a life of inward transforming.

We need to be encouraged that no matter what kind of person we are the Lord will work out His purpose of transformation in us. He is merciful, and little by little He will change us. He will transform us. I do not care for what you are outwardly or what you do outwardly, but I know there is One working within you inwardly. Praise Him for His inward working within us. He is taking every opportunity to write something of Christ within us little by little. I can testify that from observing many of the saints, more of Christ has been written into them year by year in a specific way. We need to be patient with one another in the church life because more and more of Christ is gradually being wrought into us. This is the Lord's transforming work. One person may be slow and another person may be quick in his disposition. But before the Lord there is no difference. To be fast or to be slow does not mean anything. What means something is the Lord writing Himself into our being all the time to transform us. In the age of eternity all of us will become the complete letters of Christ. At that time the entire composition of Christ will be inscribed into our whole being. Christ alone will become the very content of our mind, emotion, and will.

MIRRORS BEHOLDING AND REFLECTING
THE GLORY OF THE LORD

The second illustration in 2 Corinthians 3 is that we are mirrors beholding and reflecting the glory of the Lord. We are mirrors beholding Christ and reflecting Him, but the problem is that sometimes our heart is turned away from the Lord. Thus, we have to turn our heart to Him. Whenever our heart turns to the Lord, the veil is taken away (2 Cor. 3:16). The Lord is waiting for us to turn our hearts to Him. He is indwelling our spirit, and our spirit is the hidden man of our heart. Our heart must be turned inwardly to the indwelling Christ. Then we will behold Him and reflect Him. We have to turn our hearts to Him all the time, morning and evening, day and night. Even while we are working or driving our car, we must turn our hearts to Him. The more that we turn to Him and behold Him, the more we will reflect Him and be transformed into His image.

When we open ourselves to behold Him, He as the living Spirit imparts Himself into us. Whenever we behold the Lord, we return ourselves to the spirit. We need to look away from everything unto Jesus who is the living Spirit in our spirit. When we behold Him, He has the ground and the opportunity to impart Himself into us. This imparting of Himself into us will transform us.

When tea is added to plain water, the tea becomes mingled with the water, and the tea transforms the water in color, in expression, and in flavor. The water is in the tea and the tea is in the water. In the same way Christ is in us and we are in Christ. Just as the tea and the water are mingled together, we and Christ are mingled together. The Lord is doing a mingling and transforming work within us. The Lord's work is not a matter of outward adjustment, outward correction, or outward improvement, but a matter of Him imparting Himself into our being from within us. The more He imparts Himself into us, the more He mingles Himself with us and the more He will transform us.

We are transformed by the living Spirit. Second Corinthians 3:18 tells us that we are transformed into the same image from glory to glory even as from the Lord Spirit. He is the living Spirit within us, so we have to pay our attention to the Spirit all the time. We have to learn to open to Him. If we open ourselves to Him, He will have a way to purify us, to purge us, to saturate us, to permeate us, to fill us, to mingle Himself with us, and to transform us. Transformation takes place by this living One imparting Himself more and more into us. He imparts Himself into us by our drinking Him, eating Him, and breathing Him in. To eat Him, drink Him, and breathe Him in is to allow Him to write Himself into us, to inscribe Himself into us, by our beholding Him. He is the living Spirit waiting within us, so we need to learn to turn ourselves to the Spirit

and open to Him. Then He will saturate us, and we will be
transformed.

CHAPTER SIXTEEN

GOD'S ULTIMATE INTENTION REALIZED

Scripture Reading: Rev. 21:2-3a, 10-14, 18-23; 22:1-5; 2:7; 7:14-17; 21:6; 22:17

We have seen that God presented Himself to us as the tree of life for our enjoyment in the form of food that we may eat of Him. Throughout the whole Bible God's unique intention is that we would take Him into us and enjoy Him within as our life and everything. Eventually He will be mingled with us. The best way for something to be mingled with us is for us to eat that thing. Whatever we eat will be digested by us and will be mingled with us to be a part of us. This is the central thought of the Bible. My burden is to point out this central thought that we all might be impressed with it. This impression will revolutionize our whole Christian walk.

GOD'S INTENTION WITH THE TREE OF LIFE

In the beginning of the Bible in Genesis 2 there is a picture showing us a tree which is called the tree of life, and in front of the tree is a man of clay (vv. 8-9). Clay is the dust of the earth. With clay there is nothing precious. Beside the tree of life there was a river of water flowing and dividing into four branches, going to the four directions of the earth (v. 10). The issue of this flow was gold, bdellium, and onyx stone (v. 12). Onyx is a precious stone. Gold, bdellium, and onyx are three precious materials. There is no comparison between them and the clay.

We all must realize that God created a corporate man in Genesis 2, which included billions of persons. That man of clay was Adam, and we all are his descendants. Because we all came out of Adam, the Bible says that we are earthen vessels (2 Cor. 4:7), vessels of clay. In Genesis 2 this man of clay had nothing to do with the tree of life. He was not the gold, pearl, or onyx. But God's intention was that this. man of clay would take in the tree of life, that is, that this man would eat the tree of life. The tree of life is something living. When it gets into man, this living tree becomes a flow within, and this flow of life will transform this man of clay into precious materials (gold, bdellium, and onyx) for God's building. This is God's intention. The whole Bible of sixty-six books simply tells us this one thing—that we were made of clay but were intended by God to take Him as the tree of life. Then God who is so living will come into us as our life, and this living One who is God Himself as life to us will become a flow within us.

Right away after we were saved, after we received Christ as our life, we did have the sense that within us there was something flowing. This inner flow will carry away many things from within us, and will bring many things into us. Within our body we have the circulation of blood. Negatively, this circulation of the blood as the flow within the body carries away all the negative things, and positively, this flow of blood carries into us all the necessary nourishment and vitamins. In our physical body we have a flow, and our physical body exists by this flow.

After we received the Lord, He Himself as our life became the flow within our spirit. Now we have another flow within us besides the one in our physical body. This flow is the spiritual flow of life in our spirit, which is Christ Himself. On the negative side, this flow will carry away our bad temper, our hatred, our impatience, and our pride. On the positive side, this flow will gradually day by day bring more and more of Christ into us to nourish us, and this flowing will do a transforming work to change us, not only in position, but also in nature, in disposition.

GOD'S INTENTION IN THE GOSPEL OF JOHN

Before considering the final picture in the Bible in Revelation, we should see God's intention with life in the Gospel of John. John 1:1 and 4 say, "In the beginning was the Word, and the Word was with God, and the Word was God....In Him was life, and the life was the light of men." Verse 14 goes on to say, "And the Word became flesh and tabernacled among us." The Word was God and in this One there was life. He became flesh, walking upon this earth. At the beginning of His ministry He was recommended as the Lamb of God (1:29). Due to the fall of man the One who was life came as the Lamb of God. In Genesis 2 there was the tree of life, but afterwards in Genesis 3 there was the fall of man. Immediately after the fall of man there was a lamb (3:21).

God's intention is that He Himself would be life to man, but because man became fallen, God had to change in form from the tree of life to the Lamb. God as life came in the form of the Lamb to take away the sin of the world. According to the record of the Passover in Exodus 12, the lamb was not only good for redeeming but also good for nourishing. The blood of the lamb is for redeeming, and the meat of the lamb is for nourishing. Nourishing is something of life. Therefore, in John 1 there is the Lamb, but in chapter six there is the food, the bread of life (vv. 22-71).

Then in chapter four and chapter seven is the living water, the water of life, to drink (4:14; 7:37-38). Eventually in John 17 there is the oneness (vv. 11, 20-23). Oneness is the building. The Gospel of John starts with God Himself. God's intention is that He would be life to us. But because we became fallen, He changed in form. He became the Lamb to us to redeem us and to be food for us to eat. He is also the living water that we may drink of Him. After we eat of Him and drink of Him, eventually there is the oneness, the building.

THE TREE OF LIFE AND THE RIVER OF LIFE
IN REVELATION FOR THE TRANSFORMATION IN LIFE
AND THE BUILDING IN LIFE

In the last picture of the Bible there is a city foursquare with three gates on every side (Rev. 21:16, 12-13). Each of the twelve gates is a pearl (v. 21), and upon them are the names of the twelve tribes of Israel. This gives us a picture, telling us that all these gates are persons. They are pearls, but they all have personal names. Verse 14 speaks of the twelve foundations. The twelve foundations are precious stones, and on

them are the names of the twelve apostles. All the foundations
are persons. Peter is a foundation, and John is a foundation. Furthermore, the wall of the city is built with precious
stones (v. 18). We are not the foundations, but we are the precious stones.

In the midst of the city is a throne (22:1). Do not think that
the city of New Jerusalem is flat. It is a mountain. The height
of the wall is one hundred forty-four cubits, but the height of
the city itself is twelve thousand stadia (21:16). The city itself
is much higher than the wall. This proves that the city must
be a mountain. At the foot of the mountain the wall is built,
and on the top of the mountain there is the throne of God and
the Lamb. There are not two thrones but one throne for God
and the Lamb. Upon the throne is the Lamb, the Lamb is the
lamp, and God is the light within the lamp (v. 23). One throne
for both God and the Lamb signifies that God and the Lamb
are one. The Lamb is the lamp and God is the light within
Him. From this throne flows out the river of the water of life
winding as a spiral down the mountain. Eventually, it passes
through all the twelve gates. On either side of the river grows
the tree of life (22:2). Genesis 2 tells us that the tree of life is
good for food (v. 9), and Revelation 7:17, 21:6, and 22:17 tell us
that the water of life is good for drink. Within the city are the
water of life to drink and the tree of life to eat.

The flow of life with the tree of life as the supply transformed Peter into a precious stone. Originally, Peter was a man
of clay, but now, in the New Jerusalem, Peter becomes a precious stone. How could Peter as a man of clay be changed into
precious stone? The very God in the Lamb as the Redeemer was
received by Peter. Then out of this Lamb the water of life flowed
carrying the tree of life as the supply. Day by day, Peter ate of
the tree of life and drank of the water of life. Day by day, he
enjoyed the Triune God. By this enjoyment he was transformed
into a precious stone for God's building.

The Father is in the New Jerusalem as the source, the light.
The Son is the lamp and the tree of life. Then the Spirit is the
river of water of life (John 7:37-39). God the Father as the light
is the source. In God the Son, He comes as the Lamb to redeem
us. After we receive God the Son, the Lamb, as our Redeemer,

the water of life, the Spirit, starts to move and flow within us. Within this flow of the Spirit, is the Son, Christ as the tree of life, for us to enjoy. First, the Son as the Lamb is for us to receive as our Redeemer. After we receive Him, the flow of the Spirit will move within us, and in this flow, Christ is the tree of life as the life supply. In this way we have the three of the Triune God for our enjoyment. Now the tree of life is no longer outside of us but within us. The Lamb has been received by us, and the Triune God has been wrought into us. In Genesis 2 the tree and the flow of the water are outside of man. But in Revelation 22 the tree of life and the water of life are both in the city. Now the tree of life with the water of life have both been wrought into man.

After the tree of life and the water of life have been wrought into us, they become not only our nourishment but also the element to transform us. The more we enjoy the flow of living water within us, flowing with the tree of life as the supply, the more we will be transformed. Men of clay will be transformed into precious stones. Eventually, in the New Jerusalem, in the holy city, there will be no more clay. The entire city proper is a mountain of gold (Rev. 21:18). The entire wall is jasper, a precious stone, and all the foundations of the wall are precious stones (vv. 18-20). Furthermore, all the gates are pearls (v. 21). There are only three materials in the New Jerusalem—gold, pearl, and precious stones. By this time, all have been transformed.

In the four Gospels, is the story of Simon Peter. Many times he was shown that he was merely a man of clay. He often spoke nonsensically or acted foolishly. On the night when the Lord was betrayed, the Lord told the disciples that He would be smitten and that they would be scattered. Peter said, "If all shall be stumbled in You, I will never be stumbled" (Matt. 26:33). He spoke foolishly. Not long after that the Lord was arrested and was brought to the court of the high priest. Peter followed the Lord afar off and also entered into the courtyard of the high priest. While he sat outside in the courtyard, a maid, not a big soldier, came to him and said, "You also were with Jesus the Galilean" (v. 69). Three times

Peter denied the Lord, even with an oath. At that time Peter was certainly a mere man of clay.

However, in Acts 2—5, Peter was a transformed, shining, strong, and transparent precious stone. In these chapters he was not opaque but clear as crystal and transparent. He was precious and absolutely changed. He was not merely changed or sanctified in position, but changed in disposition. He was changed in the metabolic way. A divine "chemical element" had been put into him which caused a chemical reaction. God in the Lamb had been received by Peter, and the Spirit as the living water started to flow into him. This flow supplied him with Christ, the all-inclusive One, as the tree of life. Day by day Peter feasted on this Christ, and day by day he drank of this living water. Some heavenly chemical element was flowing into him causing a metabolic change in his very being. He became changed not only in position or form, but also in nature, disposition, and character. By this he became one of the twelve foundations of the New Jerusalem. Mere teaching or gifts cannot transform us. Only the inner life, the Triune God Himself, can transform us.

The Father is the source as the light, and the Son is the Redeemer for us to receive. If we would confess all our sins and admit and recognize that He died on the cross for our sins, right away there would be a flow within us. This is the Spirit, and within this flow is the tree of life growing in us as the life supply for us to feed upon day by day. The river of life with the tree of life are within us for us to simply drink and eat. Day by day we can receive the heavenly nourishment and all the spiritual "vitamins" can be brought into us. This will metabolically transform us. This transforming life is also a life of building. This life within not only supplies and not only transforms, but also builds us together with others.

The New Jerusalem unveils the redeeming Lamb, the flow of life, the supply of life, the transformation of life, and the building up in life. This is a picture of today's church life. The church life is composed of a group of people who realize that they are sinful and admit that God, as the source of life, loves them. In His Son He accomplished redemption, and the Son is presented to us, the sinners, as the Lamb. We confess all our sins to Him, and we admit and recognize that He is our Redeemer, the Lamb of God, who died for us to take away our sin. When we do this, right away the Spirit becomes the flow of life within us. With this flow of life, Christ is not only the Lamb but also the tree of life for us to enjoy. He is the water of life for us to drink and the tree of life for us to eat day by day. By our eating and drinking Him, the heavenly element, the divine essence and substance, is carried into us, and we are metabolically transformed to be built up with others in oneness. This building today in this age is the church and in eternity is the holy city, New Jerusalem.

This holy city is God's tabernacle, God's dwelling place. Revelation 7:15 says that we will serve God in the temple. The temple is a place not only for God to dwell in, but also for those who serve God to dwell in. Revelation 21:22 says, "And I saw no temple in it, for its temple is the Lord God the Almighty and the Lamb." This means that we will serve God in God as the temple. All the redeemed ones are the tabernacle to God for God to dwell in, and God Himself is the temple to us for us to dwell in. Eventually, God will dwell in us, and we will dwell in God. This is a mutual dwelling, a mutual habitation. While He is dwelling in us, we are dwelling in Him. This is the mingling of the Triune God with His chosen and redeemed people.

This mingling depends on the enjoyment of the Lord. We have to enjoy Him all day long by feasting on Him as the tree of life and drinking of Him as the water of life. If we are going to be transformed, built up, and mingled with the Triune God, we have to feed on Christ as the tree of life and drink of Him as the water of life day by day. May the Lord bring us into the enjoyment of Himself. May we realize that He is within us as the tree of life, supplying us all the time by the flowing of the Holy Spirit within us. We must learn how to feed on Him and how to drink of Him. Then all that He is, His element, His substance, and His essence, will be conveyed and transmitted into us. We will be transformed, built up, and mingled with the Triune God.

ABOUT THE AUTHOR

Witness Lee was born in 1905 in northern China and raised in ⹁ Christian family. At age 19 he was fully captured for Christ and immediately consecrated himself to preach the gospel for the rest of his life. Early in his service, he met Watchman Nee, a renowned preacher, teacher, and writer. Witness Lee labored together with Watchman Nee under his direction. In 1934 Watchman Nee entrusted Witness Lee with the responsibility for his publication operation, called the Shanghai Gospel Bookroom.

Prior to the Communist takeover in 1949, Witness Lee was sent by Watchman Nee and his other co-workers to Taiwan to insure that the things delivered to them by the Lord would not be lost. Watchman Nee instructed Witness Lee to continue the former's publishing operation abroad as the Taiwan Gospel Bookroom, which has been publicly recognized as the publisher of Watchman Nee's works outside China. Witness Lee's work in Taiwan manifested the Lord's abundant blessing. From a mere 350 believers, newly fled from the mainland, the churches in Taiwan grew to 20,000 in five years.

In 1962 Witness Lee felt led of the Lord to come to the United States, settling in California. During his 35 years of service in the U.S., he ministered in weekly meetings and weekend conferences, delivering several thousand spoken messages. Much of his speaking has since been published as over 400 titles. Many of these have been translated into over fourteen languages. He gave his last public conference in February 1997 at the age of 91.

He leaves behind a prolific presentation of the truth in the Bible. His major work, *Life-study of the Bible,* comprises over 25,000 pages of commentary on every book of the Bible from the perspective of the believers' enjoyment and experience of God's divine life in Christ through the Holy Spirit. Witness Lee was the chief editor of a new translation of the New Testament into Chinese called the Recovery Version and directed the translation of the same into English. The Recovery Version also appears in a number of other languages. He provided an extensive body of footnotes, outlines, and spiritual cross references. A radio broadcast of his messages can be heard on Christian radio stations in the United States. In 1965 Witness Lee founded Living Stream Ministry, a non-profit corporation, located in Anaheim, California, which officially presents his and Watchman Nee's ministry.

Witness Lee's ministry emphasizes the experience of Christ as life and the practical oneness of the believers as the Body of Christ. Stressing the importance of attending to both these matters, he led the churches under his care to grow in Christian life and function. He was unbending in his conviction that God's goal is not narrow sectarianism but the Body of Christ. In time, believers began to meet simply as the church in their localities in response to this conviction. In recent years a number of new churches have been raised up in Russia and in many eastern European countries.